~AUTHORS OF THE MIDDLE AGES~

Volume IV, Nos. 12–13

~AUTHORS OF THE MIDDLE AGES~

Historical and Religious Writers of the Latin West

General Editor: Patrick J. Geary

Volume IV, Nos. 12–13

VARIORUM
1996

AUTHORS OF THE MIDDLE AGES Vol. IV, Nos. 12–13.
Historical and Religious Writers of the Latin West: General Editor, Patrick J. Geary.

Published by VARIORUM
Ashgate Publishing Limited
Gower House, Croft Road
Aldershot, Hants GU11 3HR
UK

Ashgate Publishing Company
Old Post Road
Brookfield, Vermont 05036
USA

ISBN 0 86078 625 0

British Library Cataloguing in Publication Data
Authors of the Middle Ages. — Vol. IV, Nos. 12–13:
Historical and Religious Writers of the Latin West.
1. Fredegar—Criticism and Interpretation.   2. Gregory, I, Pope—Criticism and Interpretation.   3. Literature, Medieval—History and Criticism.   4. Latin Literature, Medieval and Modern—History and Criticism.   5. Authors, Latin (Medieval and Modern).   6. Religious Literature—History and Criticism.   I. Straw, Carole. Gregory the Great.   II. Collins, Roger. Fredegar.   III. Geary, Patrick J.
870.9'003

US Library of Congress Cataloguing in Publication Data
Gregory the Great/Carole Straw.   Fredegar/Roger Collins.
    p. cm. — (Authors of the Middle Ages: 12–13. Historical and Religious Writers of the Latin West).
Includes bibliographical references, cloth.
1. Gregory I, Pope, c. 540–604.   2. Church History—6th Century.   3. Fredergarri chronicon.   4. Franks—History—To 768.   5. France—History—to 987.   I. Straw, Carole. Gregory the Great.   II. Collins, Roger. Fredegar.   III. Geary, Patrick J.
IV. Series: Authors of the Middle Ages: 12–13.   V. Series: Authors of the Middle Ages. Historical and Religious Writers of the Latin West.
BX1076.567 1996   96–32810
270.2'092–dc20   CIP

Typeset by   Manton Typesetters,
5–7 Eastfield Road, Louth,
Lincolnshire LN11 7AJ

Printed and bound by Athenaeum Press, Ltd.,
Gateshead, Tyne & Wear.

CONTENTS

PUBLISHER'S NOTE

The two parts of this volume, *Gregory the Great* and *Fredegar* will also be available as individual paperback titles. For ease of reference, the paperback pagination appears in square brackets at the inner margins and the continuous pagination appears without brackets at the outer margins.

Gregory the Great

AUTHORS OF THE MIDDLE AGES · 12

Historical and Religious Writers of the Latin West

Gregory the Great

Carole Straw

VARIORUM
1996

AUTHORS OF THE MIDDLE AGES · 12
Historical and Religious Writers of the Latin West: General Editor, Patrick J. Geary.

Published by VARIORUM
              Ashgate Publishing Limited
              Gower House, Croft Road
              Aldershot, Hants GU11 3HR
              UK

              Ashgate Publishing Company
              Old Post Road
              Brookfield, Vermont 05036
              USA

ISBN 0–86078–429–0

First published in *Authors of the Middle Ages Vol. IV, Nos. 12–13 (Historical and Religious Writers of the Latin West)*, ed. Patrick J. Geary. Copyright © 1996 by Variorum, Ashgate Publishing Limited. ISBN 0–86078–625–0

Typeset by   Manton Typesetters,
              5–7 Eastfield Road, Louth,
              Lincolnshire LN11 7AJ

Printed and bound by Athenaeum Press, Ltd.,
Gateshead, Tyne & Wear.

CONTENTS

ABBREVIATIONS

Append	Appendix
CCL	*Corpus Christianorum Series Latina*
de gestis Langob	Paul the Deacon, *De Gestis Langobardorum*
de vir. illustr.	Isidore of Seville, *De Viris Illustribus*
Ep	*Registrum Epistularum*
HEv	*Homiliae in Evangelia*
HEz	*Homiliae in Ezechiel prohetam*
Hist. Franc.	Gregory of Tours, *Historia Francorum*
In lib. I Rg.	*In librum primum Regum expositiones*
Io. Diac. *vita Greg.*	John the Deacon, *Vita Gregorii Magni*
MGH	*Monumenta Germaniae Historica*
Mor	*Moralia in Iob Libri I–XXXV*
Paul Diac. *vita Greg.*	Paul the Deacon, *Vita Gregorii Magni*
PL	*Patrologia Latina*
RB	*Revue Bénédictine*
Reg. past.	*Regulae pastoralis liber*
SC	*Sources chrétiennes*

ACKNOWLEDGEMENTS

One of the pleasures of working on Gregory is the company of distinguished scholars. I would like to thank Robert Markus, Paul Meyvaert and Adalbert de Vogüé for their generosity in reading this manuscript and for making many valuable recommendations. I am also indebted to scholars who have worked on Gregory before me, particularly F. Holmes Dudden, whose pioneering work on Gregory has shaped generations of scholars. My deepest debt is to my husband, Frederick McGinness, whose quiet wisdom and kindness sustain me.

GREGORY THE GREAT

I. Gregory's Rome and his early life

Gregory I was pope from 590 to 604. His epithet, 'the Great', reflects the admiration of posterity for his accomplishments as a writer and theologian, as well as a pope and administrator. Gregory's books of biblical exegesis, his sermons, and treatises fundamentally shaped Christian tradition. He is considered the fourth doctor of the Church and the first exponent of a truly medieval spirituality; the Middle Ages have been termed a 'Gregorian epoque'.[1] As an administrator, Gregory was astute and highly principled, though his politics were not always successful. He was an active pope, who used the resources of the papacy to find solutions for the problems confronting the Christian community. Under Gregory's stewardship, the Roman church expanded further its role in secular affairs. In the West, Gregory is the key figure marking the transition of the papacy from late antiquity to the Middle Ages, the 'personality' that defined the age.

A world of wars, famine, and plague shaped Gregory's spirituality and his activities as pope. The city of Rome had been long in decline – like a forlorn eagle, grown bald in tribulation (*HEz.* 2.6.22). Chief of the sorrows was the deep dislocation caused by Germanic migrations. As tribes invaded the old Roman Empire, political organization deteriorated and economic instability became endemic. The last western Roman emperor, Romulus Augustulus, was deposed in 476, an event underscoring a salient trend: by this time almost the whole of the Western empire was ruled by Germanic kings. Italy's first rex, Odoacer, lasted less than 20 years. In 493, he was murdered and replaced by the Ostrogoth Theodoric. The 33 years of Theodoric's rule brought a measure of peace and prosperity to Italy, but Theodoric could not reverse the underlying direction of the Italian economy.[2] Cities and commerce continued a slow decline. While some foreign trade remained, and local markets continued to be held in the towns' *fora,* the countryside drifted further towards a natural economy of agriculture, crafts and barter. Regional economies became more distinct; transhumance and the cultivation of minor cereals become more important in an era of economic and political

---

[1] de Lubac 1959.
[2] Rouche 1986.

fragmentation. Patronage systems grew as municipal government and political life waned. Communities came to depend on local strong men (and alternatively, their bishops) for protection and advancement. Cities reflected these changes physically. Large building projects – those expressions of beneficence (εὐεργέτεια) which had helped define a civic culture – became rare. Communities had a different identity, reorganized around the fortified *castelli,* which often came to occupy the hills.

Theodoric died unable to secure his kingdom for the future, leaving Italy vulnerable to Justinian's ambitions. Determined to restore the empire to its former glory, Justinian sent out forces to reconquer the West in 535. Italy was beset with wars of various intensity for almost two decades and the peninsula suffered unparalleled destruction. Starvation and plague accompanied the wars. The population of Italy declined from approximately 5 million to 3.5 million. Desired and battered by both sides, Rome suffered especially. In 536, the Greeks attacked, but the next year Vitiges besieged the city. In 546, Rome was taken and savagely plundered by Totila, but in 547 Belisarius won the city back. Totila returned in 550, but in 552 Narses triumphed. By the time the war was over, the population of Rome had shrunk. Estimates vary widely. Perhaps the decline was from 700,000 to 200,000.[3] A low estimate of inhabitants ranges from 90,000 to 30,000.[4] In 554, Justinian issued his Pragmatic Sanction officially reuniting Italy with the empire, and ostensibly giving Rome back its traditional privileges. But the hope for peace was shattered quickly in 568, when the Lombards crossed the Alps; they continued to make trouble throughout the rest of the century. Politics in the late 5th century had three centres of power: the Lombards, the papacy, and the East as represented by the exarch of Ravenna. Often at odds with both the East and the Lombards, Gregory's papacy and the Rome it came to oversee became increasingly autonomous.

Gregory was born *circa* 540. His family was wealthy and of noble lineage and tradition, although no evidence can link him to the *gens* Anicia or Decia, as was once thought. The family estate in Rome commanded the Caelian Hill. The family also possessed properties in the neighbourhood of Rome and several farms in Sicily. Early lives of Gregory note the prominence of his ancestors in the Church. Gregory's great-great-grandfather was Bishop of Rome (Felix III, 483–92). Agapitus, who ruled the see of Peter from 535 to 536, was a distant cousin and had also resided at the family estate on the Caelian Hill. Gregory's father, Gordianus, was a *regionarius* of the Church, an office probably equivalent to that of *defensor*, having administrative and legal responsibilities. Gregory had a younger brother, Palatinus, who followed

---

[3] Rouche 1986.
[4] Pietri 1991.

Gregory in holding the office of urban prefect and is the last person recorded as holding this office for over a century – a measure both of how secular government was weakened and also of how thoroughly the papacy came to take over civic responsibilities.

The female side of Gregory's family was particularly involved with the Church and ascetic life. After the death of her husband, Gregory's mother Silvia retired to Cella Nova, near the Basilica of St Paul to live in pious seclusion. Gregory's three paternal aunts, Tarsilla, Aemiliana, and Gordiana lived at the family estate, having taken vows with varying degrees of success. While Tarsilla died in the odour of sanctity, her knees and elbows rough as camel skin from extended prayer; and while Aemiliana was also numbered among the blessed; Gordiana fell into frivolities and married the steward of her land (*HEv.* 2.38.15; *Dial.* 4.17.1–2). Gregory drew a sharp lesson from this: 'for many are called but few are chosen'.[5]

Gregory of Tours asserts that Gregory 'was so skilled in grammar, dialectic and rhetoric that he was second to none in the entire city' (*Hist. Franc.* 10.1). While education at the time was weak, Gregory was well trained. A close study of Gregory's work does reveal rhetorical training, although he was determined not to 'fetter the Divine Oracle with the rules of Donatus' (*Mor. Prae.*5). His works also reveal a knowledge of classical authors such as Seneca, Cicero, Virgil and Juvenal. However, these writers are rarely mentioned explicitly, and much classical learning may have been filtered through Ambrose and Augustine, especially. Gregory's attitude toward classical literature was cautious and, in some cases, harshly censorious. Critics see him as anti-intellectual. Certainly, Gregory reprimanded Bishop Desiderius of Vienne for lecturing on profane literature; 'the same mouth cannot sing the praises of Jupiter and the praises of Christ' (*Ep.* 11.34); but Desiderius had simply gone too far. Gregory's profession of 'learned ignorance' (cf. *Dial.* 3.37.20) was in the Augustinian tradition of preferring the simple truths of the Gospel to the deceits of pagan tradition. Gregory was not anti-intellectual, but rather he believed in the right order of things: 'the liberal arts ought to be cultivated so that through them we might gain more accurate knowledge of God's word' (*In lib. I Rg.* 5.84). Characteristic of his discretion is also his appreciation of the importance of images for the uneducated: through pictures they could read what the learned read in books (*Ep.* 9.209; 11.10). Gregory probably had training in law, considering his secular career and later letters. His works also reveal a lively interest in natural science, medicine and astronomy.

Little is known about Gregory's career before his conversion to monastic life. That he embarked upon public service is evident, and this experience

[5] Matthew 22:14.

must have shaped his later work as pope: he was accustomed to power and taking action. By 573 he was urban prefect, as *Ep*. 4.2 gives witness.[6] Gregory's conversion to monastic life came in 574, and grew from a trial he would continue to suffer throughout his life – conflicts that would become major themes of his works. Gregory was torn between his own desire to safeguard the safety of his soul in contemplative retreat and the obligation imposed upon him to serve others in public affairs. Writing to Leander of Seville in the preface to the *Moralia* in 595, Gregory reflected on his conversion. He had been displeased with himself and inspired with a desire for heavenly things long before he made a formal break with the world. At first, he attempted to reconcile his inner vocation and outward duties. He tried to serve the world in appearance only, but he found himself so entangled that he became bound also in mind and heart. Filled with great anxieties, he fled to the 'haven' of the monastery to repair what had become the 'shipwreck' of his life.

Unnerved by the incompatibility of spiritual and secular lives, Gregory's conversion expressed the need for complete abnegation to insure purity of soul. He retired from the world, establishing a monastic community dedicated to St Andrew's at Clivus Scauri, on the family estate in Rome. He created six more monasteries on family estates in Sicily, probably those dedicated to St Hermas, Sts Maximus and Agatha, St Theodore, St Hadrian, the Praetorian Monastery, and the nunnery of St Martin. However, he retained sufficient property to make later endowments to the church (cf. *MGH* 2; *Ep.* Append. 2).

Gregory spent 574–79 in the monastic community he had instituted on the family estate. Unfortunately, the solace of Gregory's monastic life was soon broken and Gregory was 'suddenly plunged into a sea of secular matters' that he found dangerous and burdensome (*Mor.* Prae. 1). Pope Pelagius II made him a deacon and then sent him to Constantinople as apocrisiarius (a papal legate) in 579. Gregory remained in Constantinople until 585–86 to represent the interests of Rome and the papacy. Part of Gregory's duties was to continue a plea for aid against the Lombards. To some extent the emperor Tiberius helped, although he was engaged in a bitter war against the Persians and could spare few troops. Gregory had less success securing aid from the emperor Maurice, who acceded in 582.

During his stay in Constantinople, Gregory was involved in contemporary theological controversies. In *Mor.* 14.56.72ff, Gregory recounted his dispute with Eutychius, the Patriarch of Constantinople, over the latter's denial of the resurrection of a truly physical body. Gregory was vindicated when Eutychius

---

[6] Alternative manuscript readings of praetor should be rejected because that office had been defunct for generations.

confessed the resurrection on his death bed in 582. It also appears that Gregory wrote the third letter for Pelagius II on the controversy over the Three Chapters when in Constantinople (*MGH* 2; *Ep.* Append. 3). This document includes several references to Greek texts unlikely to be in Rome and for which Gregory would have needed a translator.[7]

Gregory's relations with the court would prove valuable for the future. His circle of contacts was wide and gave him at least the potential for influencing the imperial government more effectively on Rome's behalf. Gregory's correspondence with members of the imperial household often reveals much personal warmth. The Empress Constantina, Theoctista – sister of the Emperor – and Narses, the patrician and general, received friendly, even intimate letters from Gregory. To the court physician, Theodorus, Gregory sent a duck with two ducklings in memory of their friendship (*Ep.* 5.46). The Emperor Maurice's cousin, Bishop Domitian of Meletinà was also among Gregory's circle of acquaintances, as were various nobles and ecclesiastics. Although as pope, Gregory came to have his differences with the Emperor in Constantinople, Gregory was cordial (and politic) enough to serve as baptismal sponsor to Maurice's and Constantina's son, Theodosius. This itself is some indication of the complicated world of political alliances and personal favours Gregory had to accommodate.

Despite his apparent success at court and with the nobility, Gregory tried to distance himself from the court and its dangerous worldly ways. He never learned Greek, and this limited his access to the bilingual society of the Byzantine court. Although Gregory's writings show familiarity with certain Greek terms, and even reveal knowledge of information only in Greek sources,[8] such knowledge could have come from intermediary sources, such as Augustine, or from the oral culture of the court at Constantinople.[9] Gregory states his ignorance of Greek in *Ep.* 7.29 and 11.55; and in another letter, Gregory refused petulantly to answer a member of the court because she had written in Greek, a language, he says he does not know (*Ep.* 3.63).

Gregory's separation from the court was indicated not only in his decision not to learn Greek, but also in his choice to live with a group of monks who had travelled with him from St Andrew's. Living in common with them and away from the court, Gregory found another safe haven. Included was Leander of Seville, a Spanish bishop, the elder brother of Isidore. Leander became a close friend, and at his request and that of other monks in the entourage, Gregory began his exposition of Job, the *Magna Moralia*. Years later, he dedicated the book to Leander.

---

[7] Meyvaert 1996.
[8] Petersen 1976.
[9] Bartelink 1994.

Pope Pelagius recalled Gregory *circa* 585–86, and Gregory returned to Rome, resuming the office of deacon and living again with his monastic community at St Andrew's. Gregory is seen to act authoritatively in the *Dialogues*, when speaking of life in '[his] monastery'. For instance, he gave orders of how the sinful monk Justus was to be treated for concealing money in violation of the rule. Gregory also forbade the brothers from attending Justus at his death, and ordered that Justus be buried with his money on a manure heap.[10] This had the desired effect on the community, and the brethren began to return even the most trifling article 'the rule' allowed them to keep (*Dial.* 4.57.8–12). On the other hand, there is no confirmation that Gregory was abbot either from his own writings or those of his contemporaries. Indeed in *Dialogues* 4.22.1, Gregory speaks of Valentio, 'who later was my abbot in my monastery here at Rome'. Gregory's authoritative behaviour vis-à-vis Justus and the monks probably stemmed from his position as founder of the community.[11]

Whether the 'rule' to which Gregory refers in this and other passages of the *Dialogues* was that of St Benedict is doubtful, principally because monastic rules were slow to circulate and gain exclusive precedence.[12] By living 'under a rule' Gregory means nothing more than living under the authority of a superior.[13] Gregory's writings, particularly his letters directing various reforms of monastic practice, give us a thorough sense of what his prescriptions for monastic life might be; they reveal, however, little of his actual life at St Andrew's. He may have continued in his work as an adviser to Pelagius. Gregory did continue to write. He edited his exposition of Job, a task he was not able to finish before his election to the papacy. The period also allowed him to make the acquaintance of monks who would later serve him as pope.

Gregory was elected to the papacy at a critical moment. In 589, Italy was inundated with floods, and the plague came in their wake. Pelagius II had succumbed to the pestilence early in 590 and the city was in turmoil. Upon his election, Gregory wrote promptly to the emperor refusing the office. Awaiting the emperor's answer, Gregory watched people dying of the disease, and pondered the wrath of God on his sinful subjects. He was determined to do something. According to a tradition going back to the seventh century, on 25 April 590 he preached a sermon in the Basilica of St John Lateran calling for repentance and reform (Greg. Tur. *Hist. Franc.* 10.1; Paul Diac. *vita Greg.* 11; Io. Diac. *vita Greg.* 1.41). 'Let the punishments we already suffer break up the hardness of our hearts ... [T]he people were smitten by God's

---

[10] Cf. Acts 8:20.
[11] Cf. Brechter 1939; Richards 1980.
[12] Hallinger 1957.
[13] de Vogüé 1966.

wrath ... [but] let none despair of the greatness of his sins ... The good and merciful God desires that pardon should be claimed from Him by prayers', was Gregory's message. He then led a penitential procession with legates from the major churches in Rome toward the Basilica of St Maria Maggiore. According to legend, Gregory saw a dazzling vision of the archangel Michael at the top of Hadrian's tomb: God had heard their prayers, and the archangel was returning his flaming sword of vengeance into his scabbard. Today, a statue of Michael on the Castel Sant'Angelo commemorates this legend.

On 3 September 590, Gregory was consecrated pope. Gregory's anxieties and misgivings about his election appear in the early correspondence of his papacy. He was not up to the task: 'You call an ape a lion' he complained to Narses (*Ep*. 1.6). In *Ep*. 1.5 to Theoctista, the theme of active and contemplative lives which so animates the *Moralia* appears in its bleakest form of conflict. Because of the busyness of secular activities, he has lost the joys of inward tranquillity. Although he has loved Rachel, by God's mysterious judgement, he has been wed to Leah and now must serve with her. Gregory feared his spiritual security would be undermined, for 'what the mind has not accepted willingly, it cannot control fittingly and harmoniously'.

The temptations of the secular world were no mere literary topoi – some truly *were* tempting. Though Gregory's conscious intent was to reject worldly affairs and hold himself far above them, beneath his contempt lay a secret attraction: 'little by little we become accustomed to his very speech which is unworthy of us, and we even cling to these things with pleasure so that we are no longer willing to relinquish them'. Although we enter service 'against our will, from condescension' (*Dial*. 3.15.16) soon we move from 'frivolous errors to culpable guilt' (*Dial*. 3.15.16). Worldly involvement could easily subvert self-discipline, and the soul would slide uncontrollably into sin. When Gregory condemned the pride of the bad ruler in *Moralia* 34.23.52, he described a hypocrite as one who '[sought] to be compelled to do what he secretly long[ed] for'.

The dangers of worldly life – one's vulnerability to life's attractions, despite one's conscious intent – made engagement in the world a sacrifice of the very purity one longed for in one's heart. Paradoxically, to undertake worldly duties as a sacrifice of obedience to God could actually perfect the soul: thus, the spiritual crisis that so threatened to destroy Gregory's life had a possible resolution. The Christian could serve the needs of others in the world, for conscious of his own sin, he might grow in compunction and penitence, and become more perfect in humility.[14]

When Gregory became pope in 590, he was challenged even more to find a way to keep that spiritual equilibrium. He found reconciliation. In society,

[14] Straw 1988.

the two ways of life, the more spiritual and the more carnal, were mysteri-
ously mixed: 'I suspect there is no Abel without Cain for a brother', Gregory
opined. The righteous were compelled to live among the reprobate, like Job
becoming the 'brother of dragons and the friend of ostriches' (*Ep.* 11.27).[15]
Though mingling with sinners, the righteous must find a way to retain their
sense of separateness and virtue. In society, they were compelled to live
among carnal sinners, even as individually, they were forced to integrate carnal
activity and spiritual contemplation in their own lives. The Christian needed
to have *discretio*, the discernment that weighed (*pensare*) all decisions and
actions carefully, moderating them according to the rule. Following the 'line
of discretion' (*linea discretionis*), the good Christian would balance his behaviour preserving a mean between extremes. Being neither too severe, nor
too lax; neither too self-centered in solitude, nor too involved in a deadening
world, Christians could positively integrate activity and contemplation in their
own lives. And on a larger scale, they could find for themselves a place in
the concord of the Church and the world that profited both themselves and
their neighbours.

   Discretio was the key virtue of the pragmatic pope Gregory, for it made
action and accommodation possible. Based on a realistic assessement of possibilities, discretion fostered a creative flexibility that enabled Gregory to make
the most advantageous (and moral) choices. Gregory's command, '*Age quod
agis*', 'do what you're doing, don't let your hand or feet stop working', carried a certain determined urgency (*HEv.* 2.37.9; *Dial.* 4.58.1). By using discretion to adjust rules to circumstance, Paul 'turned back to the ministry of
faith, what he did unfaithfully, so to speak. For many times a virtue is lost
when clung to indiscreetly; and held the more strongly when discreetly
intermitted' (*Mor.* 28.11.29). This political acumen, reminiscent of the Roman patron and aristocrat that he was, would serve Gregory well as pope.

II.   Gregory's activities as Bishop of Rome

Securing Rome

The first years of Gregory's papacy are remarkable for their literary produc-
tions alone, quite apart from his dealing with the Lombards and his attempts
to set the Church in order. Shortly after Gregory became pope, he wrote to
Leander and promised to send the *Moralia* (*Ep.* 1.41, April 591), but he sent
the manuscript with a dedicatory letter to Leander in 595 or later (*Ep.* 5.53).
Mulling over the problems he faced as pastor and *rector*, Gregory wrote
Regulae pastoralis liber between September 590 and February 591, and dedi-

---

[15] Job 30:29, this is how Gregory read it.

cated it to John of Ravenna. John had chastized him for seeking to avoid office, and Gregory must have taken this criticism very seriously. Gregory gave a blueprint for the good ruler: the qualities he must possess, and how exactly he should exercise power to achieve his goals. One might see the work as a therapeutic form of self-direction. Later it would serve many others faced with the practical difficulties of how to assert authority and persuade recalcitrant minds. Gregory's preoccupation with these issues of governing souls was further manifest in a synodical letter written to John of Constantinople and the other eastern patriarchs in February 592 (*Ep.* 1.24). Much of this letter echoes closely the *Regulae pastoralis liber.*

Gregory also undertook preaching homilies on Ezechiel in 591–92, even as the political situation in Rome grew more urgent. In the absence of effective secular government, Gregory moved the Church towards filling this vacuum of power and leadership; and he advanced arguments justifying the Church's role in the world that would be useful for later generations. For Gregory, the Church's right to possess secular power was evident in the conversion of the world to Christianity. No longer need the Church suffer the adversity of persecutions to prove its holiness. Only hypocrites argued that. On the contrary, the Church could enjoy prosperity and temporal power and still preserve her holiness (*Mor.* 26.26.44–26.42.77; *Mor.* 13.41.46). The problem lay in knowing *how* to exercise power correctly, ' [f]or power is good in its proper place, but it requires careful conduct in a ruler' (*Mor.* 26.26.45). Guided by God, leaders of the Church could be expected to possess the discretion needed to exercise power correctly and help advance God's plans for the Church in the world.

The Lombards presented a host of problems that tested such a philosophy of right rule. With the centre of the Byzantine government in Ravenna with the exarch, the south fell outside its realm of true interest. With ineffective *magistri militum* stationed in Rome, and what would later become the duchy, Gregory often assumed their duties. Hedged in by Lombard dukes at Spoleto and Benevento, Gregory felt that he had not been made 'bishop of the Romans, but of the Lombards, whose treaties are swords and whose favour is a punishment' (*Ep.* 1.30). The exarch of Ravenna ignored his plight, indeed, Gregory complained that the sedition of imperial soldiers pressed him more heavily than the swords of the Lombard outside (*Ep.* 1.3). The situation was critical. The plague of 590–91 had been followed by drought and famine. Troops were unpaid and restive.

In 591, while Gregory was preaching on Ezechiel and writing the *Regulae pastoralis liber*, the dukes of Spoleto and Benevento died and were replaced by Ariulf and Arichis respectively. While the new Lombard king, Agilulf, busied himself repressing rebellions, Ariulf took up arms. Gregory took care of Roman interests. He authorized Peter the Subdeacon to buy grain

for the Roman population ravaged by famine and plague (*Ep.* 1.70). Gregory
sent troops to the *magister militum*, Velox, and advised the other *magistri*
Maurilius and Vitalianus on strategies to employ against Ariulf (*Ep.* 2.4, 2.27,
2.28). To create a line of defence, Gregory appointed the *vir clarissimus*
Leotinius to defend Nepi, and he sent the tribune Constantius to defend
Naples when the exarch refused to appoint anyone (*Ep.* 2.10, 2.47). In 592,
Suana surrendered and Ariulf took a string of cities as he advanced on and
laid siege to Rome. Gregory reacted with a personal sense of fear and sad-
ness, believing as he did that the Lord chastized both the ruler and his
people through the adversities he sent: the *flagella dei*. Because of his own
sins, Gregory said, Ariulf had invaded the city, killing some citizens and
mutilating others. Gregory had fallen ill from grief (*Ep.* 2.38).

Naples as well as Rome was threatened by the exarch's inactivity (cf. *Ep.*
2.38). Ignored by the emperor, Gregory was eventually forced to become the
paymaster, defraying the daily expenses of defending the city of Rome (cf. *Ep.*
5.39). In July 592, when the exarch Romanus did not respond to Gregory's
call for peace with the Lombards, Gregory took the extraordinary action of
concluding a treaty with Ariulf, paying him with Church funds to withdraw
from Rome (cf. *Ep.* 2.38). Gregory had saved the city from being sacked.

Meanwhile, the exarch continued with own plans. Byzantine strategies were
designed to protect Ravenna; a peace between Rome and the duke of Spoleto
could threaten Ravenna. The exarch soon launched a counter-attack on Ariulf,
retaking Roman cities and entering Rome long enough to garner the remain-
ing troops for the defence of Perugia and Narni. He then returned to defend
Ravenna. Gregory felt betrayed, 'Rome was abandoned so that Perugia might
be garrisoned' (*Ep.* 5.36).

Response to Lombard losses came not from Ariulf, but from King Agilulf,
who moved south from Pavia in 592–93, recapturing Perugia and then be-
sieging Rome. Gregory alluded to Agilulf's siege in his *Homilies on Ezechiel*
2. Praefatio; 2.6.24; and 2.10.24. Anguished by the destruction of the city
and its people, Gregory ended his homilies abruptly, quoting Job: 'My soul
is weary of my life'.[16] He continued in explanation,

> When life itself is lost, how can one find pleasure in declaring the mystic
> meaning of Holy Scripture? And when can I offer others sweet drinks if daily
> I am forced to drink bitter potions? What, therefore, remains except that we
> thank God with tears amidst the scourges we suffer for our sins (*HEz.*
> 2.10.24).

The Lombards soon departed. In a subsequent letter, Gregory referred to himself as a paymaster of the Lombards, whose swords were held back only by

---

[16] Job 10:1.

daily ransom from the Church. The cost to live among them was impossible to compute (*Ep.* 5.39).

While the Lombard problem was acute in the first years of his papacy, Gregory did address other problems facing the Church, and he continued to write. In 593, he preached his Homilies on the Gospels to the clergy and people of Rome. Apparently he was so ill that a secretary had sometimes to read his sermons. Gregory began a work of miracles of the Italian Fathers, and the *Dialogues* were published in 594. The *Dialogues* show the brutality of the Lombards and the fear they inspired. Their quickness to kill the innocent, their taking of captives, their sacrilegious worship of idols, and various other acts of violence are a continuous undercurrent of the book. The book was designed to reassure the doubtful not only of the power of saints and the reality of the invisible world beyond, but also of the power of the Church through its leaders – its bishops and abbots – and its sacraments to safeguard a troubled society and shepherd its people to their promised reward. The Church had a comforting power, and the devil was reduced to his true pettiness, punning 'Maledict' when he called upon Saint Benedict.

During 595, Gregory watched impatiently as the exarch Romanus entered into peace negotiations with Agilulf, and threatened to conclude his own peace if none were forthcoming from Ravenna. He was aware that this would mean the ruin of various islands and other places (cf. *Ep.* 5.34), but he was as committed to preserving Rome as the exarch was to preserving Ravenna. Gregory informed Emperor Maurice that Agilulf was ready to make peace, and this news was not well received. Obviously, the Byzantine government would not want to see Rome allied with the Lombard king, encircling Ravenna with Germans or their allies. Gregory's relations with the emperor hit a low point. Maurice called Gregory a fool, saying he was merely deceived by Agilulf. Gregory's sarcasm deflected the insult: indeed, he had to have been a fool to stand by and endure the Lombards while the Emperor did nothing. Gregory defended his actions to preserve Rome and sharply reminded Maurice of his duty to rule over priests in a manner that paid them due reverence (*Ep.* 5.36).

Gregory's lack of faith in the imperial authorities led him to get involved in the peace negotiations, a move that led to placards of protest in Ravenna. Gregory excommunicated those responsible, an action that was more symbolic than practicable, for the exarch Romanus was probably behind the campaign. Gregory again impeached Byzantine administration: he suffered more from the malice of Romanus and state officials than he did from the swords of the Lombards (*Ep.* 5.40, 5.42). His disillusionment with the Byzantine administration must have been profound. Gregory was preoccupied with conditions in Rome: ransoming hostages, securing the grain supply when famine threatened, distributing pay to unruly imperial soldiers, and supplying the needs of refugees. The exarch Romanus died in 596, and the Lombard duke, Arichis, took the opportunity to raid Campania and the Abruzzi.

At last, in 598, Gregory's representative, the abbot Probus, arranged a peace with Agilulf, this time with the support of the new exarch Callinicus (cf. *Ep*. 9.11). Peace was formalized in 599, but lasted only two years, and the plague returned (during 599) to mar even that respite. Gregory again felt the nearness of the world's end (*Ep*. 9.232), and now also of his own death. Since 598, gout had made movement excruciating; he continued his regimen of fasting. His body was 'dried up, as though already in the tomb'; he longed for death as 'the only possible remedy for [his] sufferings' (*Ep*. 9.20).

Not only had the Byzantine government failed to be of assistance during the Lombard wars, they had also rejected Gregory's call to repress the so-called Donatists in Africa. The Byzantine government had sided with the patriarch of Constantinople in the dispute over his title 'Ecumenical Patriarch', and they had failed to support Gregory in other disputes, such as the disputed election to the episcopal see of Salona. While Gregory might not have wished to break with the Byzantine government, he did begin to pay more attention to Germanic rulers. His correspondence with them becomes more frequent after 595. Gregory's frustrations were not limited to the Greeks, however. He even had trouble securing obedience from the bishop of Ravenna, a personal friend, on the issue of the pallium.

During the years of uncertain peace negotiations with the Lombards, between 595 and 598, Gregory had spent much time teaching the monastic community around him. He preached on Proverbs, the Prophets, the Heptateuch, the Song of Songs, and the first book of Kings – enormous enterprises. In the surviving works, his commentaries on the Song of Songs, and the first book of Kings, one finds great longing for the contemplative life. The Song of Songs is devoted to the pursuit of mystical knowledge, and while *In lib. I Reg.* has the typical concern for the preacher and the active and contemplative lives, much time is devoted to the inner workings of monastic life. *In lib. I Reg.* was corrected in the last years of his life and is the final exegetical work we have from his pen.

To Gregory, the secular world offered little but disorder and misery. The Byzantine government renewed the war in 601. The exarch of Ravenna continued to be more of a problem than a solution. When the exarch Callinicus captured Agilulf's daughter and her husband paraded them in triumph, the infuriated Lombards retaliated by allying with the Avars. When Cremona and Mantua fell, and Ravenna seemed next, Callinicus was recalled. His successor Smaragdus concluded a peace in 603 which lasted until 605. Gregory was thus able to spend his final year enjoying a respite from the depredations of the Lombards and the machinations of the imperial government.

Gregory's dealings with the Lombards reveal pragmatism and courage and are a good index to the temporal power of the papacy. He did make some effort at reproachment. He corresponded with Agilulf's wife Theudelinda, and he did succeed in securing some tolerance for Catholic subjects. The Queen's son was baptised a catholic, an important step in bringing the Lombards into the fold. Gregory's independent initiatives with the Lombards reveal the vulnerability of the imperial government. With the Byzantine power base in Ravenna, they needed to marshal their military forces to defend the imperial city. The government lacked the resources to defend the south, and the southern cities were left to their own devices. Gregory resented the choice of priorities and faulted the imperial government for abandoning Rome to the barbarians, but stopped short of making a complete break with imperial authorities; indeed, he continued to try to make them see the pressing needs of Rome and Italy. While his actions at the beginning of his papacy were energetic in trying to secure peace with the Lombards, in the later years of his papacy, he left matters in the hands of the exarch of Ravenna.

Gregory's concern was for Rome, and Gregory must be credited with helping preserve Rome by undertaking successfully the various responsibilities that normally befell secular rulers, including twice saving the city from being sacked by the Lombards.

The Roman Church and reform

One sees a complicated society reflected in Gregory's early works and letters. In Rome and Italy, political instability and economic decline created a society of vertiginous fluidity. The late sixth century experienced a social revolution.[17] Civilian government weakened, and in Rome, the senatorial aristocracy faded in influence and power. Many leading families had migrated to Constantinople or elsewhere during the Gothic wars. The Senate had ceased to function effectively soon after the reconquest, and early in the seventh century the *curia senatus* was turned into the Church of St Adriano, a measure of changing times and values. Increasingly, the Church took over secular responsibilities, particularly those pertaining to public welfare and safety. As a measure of this shift from secular to ecclesiastical authority, one finds bishops assuming the garb of senators and jealously guarding the privilege of wearing them. The decline of the senatorial aristocracy and its civic commitments was reflected also in building patterns. Patronage focused around small foundations associated with churches and charitable institutions, with considerable attention paid only to large intramural churches and the cem-

---

[17] Brown 1984; Llewellyn 1970.

etery churches devoted to martyrs.[18] Despite the optimistic provisions of Justinian's Pragmatic Sanction for restoring Rome, only the Porta Salaria was rebuilt in 565. On the whole, secular structures were allowed to decay.

As the traditional civilian senatorial aristocracy faltered, a vigorous new military élite arose to challenge the Church's expansion into the world. One finds a lack of division between civil and military power after the Gothic War and in the sixth century, as Brown notes: 'In practice civil and military spheres overlapped continually, but most of the pressures worked against the autonomy of the state power'.[19] A new military aristocracy came to dominate society at the expense of the civilian senatorial aristocracy, and Gregory's policies attempted to establish the Church as a counterweight to this military élite and its ambitions. Gregory's letters and the *obiter dicta* in his exegetical works reveal a word of mercurial mobility, of brazen usurpation of the property, rights, authority and even the regalia of others.

Given his own personal struggles against the dangers of secular life, Gregory was especially sensitive to those who sought to find a career and worldly success in the Church. Such carnal-minded Christians had no place in the Church. Gregory cautioned against using such unseasoned wood 'unless dried of their humors', for such 'newness' could destabilize the Church. In a simile suggesting parallel and competitive hierarchies, Gregory argued that bishops must be trained thoroughly, just as generals are trained before commanding troops (*Ep*. 5.58, 9.219, 5.60). The Church had its own generals, army, and soldiers fighting for spiritual goals and they were very different from those men who held sway in the world.

Wary of the abuses of laymen and the dangers of secular life in general, Gregory continued the practice begun in Constantinople of living a monastic life while serving as pope. His biographer, John the Deacon (*vita Greg*. 2.12), writes that Gregory lived in common with his *familia* of monks and clerics in the Lateran palace in such a manner that the Church of Rome resembled the Church of the Apostles. Certainly, his life was disciplined. Gregory continued his ascetic practices; his one indulgence a fondness for *cognidium*, a wine from Alexandria, flavoured with resin. His dress was monastic, although on public occasions he preserved the dignity of his office: he did not hesitate to complain when sent an inferior nag and asses to ride in procession (*Ep*. 2.50).

Most important was the circle of friends he assembled to help him: trusted monks and clerics who displaced the prevailing clergy. Gregory knew that 'many secular things [were] done under the dress of sanctity' and wanted to be assured of the sincerity of his administrators (*Ep*. 7.29). Peter the

[18] Ward-Perkins 1970, 45ff.
[19] Brown 1984, 9.

Subdeacon (and later Deacon) administered Sicily and was probably a friend from St Andrew's. Gregory cast this 'most beloved son' as interlocutor of the *Dialogues*. Aemilianus and Paterius were clerics who served as notaries, as was John, who served as a *defensor*. Maximianus had been Abbot of St Andrew's and later became Bishop of Syracuse and vicar in Sicily. Marinianus, another monk from St Andrew's, became Bishop of Ravenna. The monk Claudius become Abbot of Sts John and Stephen in Classis. Claudius visited Gregory in the mid-nineties and took the notes of Gregory's sermons on the Song of Songs and the first book of Kings which have come down to us.

The 'monasticization' of Gregory's administration led to a decline in the prerogative of clerics: monks were employed in the *familia* of the Lateran and in the administration of the patrimony, the archdeaconate was diminished, the churches were removed from the care of the priestly colleges of the *tituli* to that of the communities of monks.[20]

With this core of supporters, Gregory hoped to establish a Church purified of various abuses of worldliness. At the very beginning of his papacy, letters to Peter the Subdeacon and others indicate Gregory's determination to end various abuses (cf. *Ep*. 1.9, 1.18, 1.23, esp. *CCL* Append. 1). Gregory was an active reformer, albeit through the day-to-day policies of his pontificate, but these quotidian actions were what mattered most.

Gregory succeeded in holding only one synod, at St Peter's in 595. Twenty-three bishops from the suburban provinces attended, while the bishop of Ravenna absented himself (*MGH, Ep*. 5.57a). Present also were 35 priests of titular churches, and the Roman clergy. Six reforms were promulgated; most concern details of internal organization. More substantive reforms were decreed. Lay attendants were excluded officially from the service of the pope in the Lateran palace, formalizing Gregory's own policy of surrounding himself with monks and select clergy. Rectors of the patrimony of the Church were forbidden to affix titles of ownership on estates they felt belonged to the Church. Gregory's letters frequently address such crimes of usurpation committed by ecclesiastical authorities as well as by laymen. Gregory wanted equity and order: 'We want neither to lose property nor to take it unjustly', he asserted (*Ep*. 1.63). However, Gregory did allow ecclesiastical property to devolve into private hands through inherited succession (cf. *Ep*. 9.236), and he would hedge difficulties by saying discreetly: 'some are to be submitted to while they steal from us, but others are to be prevented, without violation of charity, not from anxiety lest they take away our goods, but lest they ruin themselves by stealing what is not their own' (*Mor*. 31.13.22). Another re-

---

[20] Penco 1959; Llewellyn 1974. Other changes will be seen below in the synodical decrees of 595.

form tried to limit corruption and secular influence in a specific way. The payment of fees for ordination, conferral of the pallium, or the preparation of charters for these acts was forbidden.[21] Finally, slaves were to be allowed to become monks, a strategy that would have strengthened the manpower of the Church at the expense of secular lords.

Gregory made some minor changes in liturgical practices, apparently reflecting his experience in Constantinople (cf. *Ep.* 9.26). He was most important for the reorganization and adaptation of the eucharistic prayer: the modification of the litany of the Kyrie, the insertion of the Pater Noster at the end of the canon, an addition to the prayer 'Hanc Igitur', and the extension of the chanting of the Alleluia outside of Easter, except during Lent.

Gregory's letters provide a more accurate measure of his success and the progressiveness of his policies as pope than do the reforms of his synod of 595 or those of the liturgy. If usurpation, disorder, and the corruption characterized the secular world, these same problems are evident in the Church Gregory directed. While Gregory sought to set the Church on a clearer course, those same problems affected the Church deeply and he had mixed success in his pursuits.

Governing the patrimony

Much of Gregory's daily life was spent dealing with the administration of the papal patrimony, and it is perhaps in this that Gregory achieved most. The historian Dudden believed that Gregory deserved the epithet 'the Great' for his astute management of estates: under him estates increased in value, tenants were prosperous, and revenues poured into the treasury.[22] The prosperity of the patrimony can be inferred from the programmes of social welfare extended to the Roman population during the Lombard invasions, and the substantial ransoms paid to the Lombards themselves. Evident from Gregory's correspondence are a careful attention to detail and an equanimity of judgement that suggest he had had considerable administrative practice before his election to the papacy. He appears to have had two economic goals: to better production in order to accumulate provisions; and to provide justice to the peasants so that they would be interested in cultivating the land.[23] He is progressive and innovative. He will seek reform, and yet accommodate when necessary.

Gregory directly oversaw the papal patrimony consisting of between 1360 and 1800 square miles divided into estates in Italy; in the islands of Sicily,

---

[21] Payment for burials in consecrated ground had been outlawed previously.
[22] Dudden 1905, 1, 20.
[23] Rouche 1986.

Sardinia, Corsica; and in the extra-Italian territories of Africa, Gaul, and Dalmatia. The Church inherited the late antique economic unit of the great estate worked by labourers and slaves. Individual estates of the patrimony were either farmed directly by the Church, leased out to wealthy tenants on lifetime leases (*emphyteuses*), or on fixed-term leases to lesser men (*conductores*). These overseers were essentially farmers themselves. Along with poorer labourers (*rustici*) and slaves (*servi*), serfs (*coloni*) worked on the estates under the supervision of the *conductor*.

Gregory aimed to reform abuses in the administration of the estates, and assure their efficient management. To this end, he appointed *rectores* or *defensores* to oversee the estates. These were incorporated into a college, or *schola*, headed by a *primicerius* ; the seven senior *defensores* were given titles of *regionarii*. Each defensor had a staff of bailiffs and agents (*actores*; *actionarii*) who were also tonsured, another sign of Gregory's desire to keep the Church as free as possible from corruptible secular men. Yet the very fluidity of society made possible the growth of impostors who claimed to be *defensores* and tried to levy exactions against bishops and peasants (cf. *Ep.* 1.68, 9.22).

The letters reveal the plight of the *coloni*, and the abuses of the powerful (including unscrupulous *defensores*). Gregory attempted to mitigate the conditions of the less fortunate even as he strove for efficient management of the estates. Success was difficult to achieve. We read of complaints that agents of the Roman church were corrupt (cf. *Ep.* 1.71, 9.40, 5.33, 1.53, 9.193, 9.84; *CCL* Append.1) and agents of other churches just as oppressive (*Ep.* 8.3, 9.145, 9.146). In Sicily, nobles and the Praetor mistreated the poor, and Gregory charged Peter the Subdeacon to rectify the situation. His advice was a characteristic statement of discretion: 'Be submissive to them when they act rightly, but stand up in opposition when they act wrongly. But so act that neither your humility be lax, nor your authority unbending, but let justice season your humility and humility soften your justice' (*CCL* Append.1).

Gregory had to deal with some powerful leaders who were little better than thick-skinned thugs, such as Theodore, the duke of Sardinia. To have any influence, one needed both to acknowledge the power of such strong men, and yet be brave enough to point out their failings. Such were the practical strategies of ruling souls put forward in the *Regulae pastoralis liber*, but admittedly, more was often needed than acute psychology. In Theodore's case, Gregory appealed to Theodore's immediate superior, the exarch of Africa, Gennadius, and he asked the deacon, Honoratus, Gregory's delegate (*apocrisiarius*) in Constantinople, to present the case of Theodore's crimes to Emperor Maurice himself (*Ep.* 1.47, 1.59). Letters in 595 and 603 reveal that nothing had changed in Sardinia (*Ep.* 5.38, 14.2). Exactions were so heavy that parents were selling their children into slavery; paganism flourished at the price of a bribe – all this because the duke had to raise what he had paid to attain his office (the *suffragium*).

Gregory could do little to affect the maladministration of a government in which patronage and *suffragia* were structural realities. His repeated calls for reform of simoniacal practices in almost every jurisdiction reveal the depth and intractability of systemic problems. His plaintive appeals to Theoctista, the emperor's sister, or to other members of court about political matters show both Gregory's lack of effective direct power, and also his entanglement in the web of personal patronage systems characteristic of late antique government and, later, of feudalism in general. Gregory himself participated in gift-giving and providing *douceurs* to the powerful (cf. *CCL* Append.1; *Ep.* 3.5). He commended people for office, albeit with the proviso 'in so far as justice allows' (cf. *Ep.* 11.4). He protected acquaintances from prosecution for corruption, the most notorious being Libertinus, the ex-praetor of Sicily who was wanted by the Byzantine government for various crimes (*Ep.* 11.4). Nothing existed as an alternative to patronage systems; one could only hope to make them work properly. Charges of bribery, simony and corruption resulted when abusive people attained positions of power; one hoped to place them with good men (i.e., ecclesiastics, or pious laymen). Political reform depended on personal reform.

The abuses of the estate system is recorded in the lives of the peasants. Gregory's behaviour was progressive by sixth-century standards. In letter 1.53, Gregory expresses the purpose of governing 'not so much to promote the worldly interests of the Church as to relieve the poor in their distress and especially to protect them from oppression'. His letters generally testify to this policy; especially important is letter 1.42 to Peter the Subdeacon. Gregory forbade the collection of exorbitant marriage fees (1.42); he recognized the marriage of serfs as valid (*Ep.* 9.46). Since the prevailing practice of granting lands by a 29 year contract threatened the labourers with eviction, Gregory replaced the contract with a *libellus*, allowing land to be inherited (cf. *Ep.* 1.42). With this innovation, Gregory sought to reverse a trend which had long weakened the economy: the tendency of farmers to abandon the land and cause a lowering of production. This hereditary grant of land anticipates medieval practices of land use.

The peasants had other worries. Taxes were exacted with unfair weights and measures, peasants were forced to supply grain at disadvantageous market prices, and often they had to pay for grain lost in shipment to Rome (*Ep.* 1.42, 13.35). Gregory sought to rectify these practices by correcting weights, regulating prices, and restricting liability for lost grain. The Church collected a wide range of taxes, tributes, and imposts originally levied by the imperial government. Gregory sought to have these compounded into a lump sum, whose payment would be regulated by charters of security to prevent overtaxation (*Ep*. 1.42, 13.35). The land tax, or *buratio,* collected by the Church for the imperial government thrice yearly was especially odious. Gregory's actions here were innovative; he prevented the borrowing of money at exorbitant rates to pay for these taxes by having the Church advance payment (*Ep*. 1.42, 13.35).

Other acts also underscore Gregory's concern for the poor. Gregory insisted that monies *conductores* had gained illegally be redistributed to the poor (*Ep*. 13.37). His charitable donations in Rome reached bureaucratic proportion: he kept systematic records of the poor (listing name, age, sex, address, occupation) and the gifts they had received. These were still preserved in the Lateran archives in the time of John the Deacon (cf. *vita Greg*. 2.30). These donations took the place of the imperial annual income on produce (*annonae)* and were more varied and generous. Each month wheat, rice, cheese, lard, fish and oil were distributed to the needy. Gregory's generosity to the poor became legendary. Both the deacons Paul and John record that Gregory left the papal treasury nearly bankrupt (cf. Io. Diac. *vita Greg*. 4.5; Paul Diac. *vita Greg*. 29). While this may be hyperbole, the letters do reveal Gregory in the role of munificent patron. He gave subsidies and various gifts to individuals in need who petitioned him and he often granted donations to support monasteries, nunneries, hospitals and churches. Gregory may have succeeded in making the Church itself appear to be the beneficent patron. Slaves fled from laymen, Gregory noted, and from the estates of monasteries. But none left the estates of the Roman church. Instead, fugitives would seek asylum in Rome's holy churches (*Ep*. 1.39; 3.1).

Gregory's treatment of the Jews reflects the prejudices of his age. Under civil law, the Jews were taxed heavily and excluded from military and civilian offices. Jews were punished more strictly than Christians, particularly for 'insults' against Christians. Practice of their religion was frequently hindered, and in the case of Frankish Jews, some were compelled to be baptized. Gregory's policy was a mixture of severity and 'persuasion'. A Jewish synagogue within hearing distance of a church had to be compelled to move (*Ep*. 2.6), and the Jews who had converted Christians were to be punished (*Ep*. 3.37). Following tradition, Gregory felt it was the Biblical prophecy of Christians to convert the Jews, and for that reason he ordered the subdeacon Anthemius to assist them 'with reasonable moderation' lest they suffer from want of food (*Ep*. 4.31). Other actions were less charitable, and adversely affected the economic status of the Jews. On declaring their Christianity, slaves were to have full claim to freedom. Their masters could not sell them. The only exception was for slaves brought recently from foreign markets, who must be sold to Christian masters (*Ep*. 4.21, 6.29). Escaped slaves should not be returned but given sanctuary (*Ep*. 4.9). But Jewish creditors were not to be defrauded of debts (*Ep*. 1.42). And Gregory

forbade Jews to be oppressed or vexed unreasonably; they were protected
by Roman law (*Ep.* 2.45).

Persuasion took the form of economic advantage. Conversion would win
remission of dues on estates. Even if parents proved to be non-practising
Christians, the children would be brought up as Catholics (*Ep.* 2.50; 5.7).
Gregory opposed forced baptism. Those brought to the font 'more by com-
pulsion than by the sweetness of preaching' were likely to relapse into superstition (*Ep.* 1.45). To Januarius, he counselled moderation. The will to resist
would not be stirred up; they must not be forced to conversion (*Ep.* 9.196).

Gregory's policy toward the Jews appears lenient when compared to that
directed against rural pagans. Peasants were to be forced to give up their
indigenous religion by ruthless measures. In Sardinia, a notoriously wild and
heathen island, the *coloni* on church estates were to have their dues increased
until starvation forced them to submit (*Ep.* 4.26).

III. The Pope and the Church universal

With his own power base in Rome and the papal patrimony, Gregory's dealings with other churches needed to be calculated carefully. The bishops of
other cities had their own bases of power, their own senses of autonomy and
their own ambitions. The Catholic church in the late sixth century did not
have a clear and cogent hierarchical order with Rome at the helm, and there
is no evidence that Gregory had such a vision for the Church. The provenance
of Gregory's authority was limited. When called upon to forward an imperial law to the bishops 'within the writ', Gregory contacted bishops in Italy,
Sicily, Sardinia, Greece, and the Balkans (*Ep.* 8.10) – a small sphere, omitting Africa, much of the East and the North.

Nor were Gregory's claims ambitious. He asserted Rome's right to judge
in certain moral issues, for Peter was first among the apostles, and his see
held this authority. But Gregory made no broad claims of Roman primacy,
as is later understood by the term. Bishops were subject to the Holy See when
they committed a fault, 'but when no fault exacts this submission, all are
equal by the law of humility', Gregory wrote (*Ep.* 8.29). To maintain both
the equality of churches and the authority of Rome to 'bind and loose' was
a flexible position, allowing considerable discretion. Respect for Gregory's
advice on moral issues was by no means a foregone conclusion. When possible, Gregory tried to enlist secular authorities to further his aims, but as
often as not, this led to frustration.

A pattern emerges of Gregory's early activity reforming the Church, followed by a period of his adjustment to the limits of his effective power.
Gregory did learn from experience and change.

Africa

Generally, Gregory was most successful closer to Rome. The further away, the weaker was his power, and the less accurate his knowledge, despite his use of informants.[24] Africa was a case in point. Gregory failed to win against the Donatists; he chose a losing battle. The Donatists of the sixth century were not those of Augustine's time. They did not rebaptize members nor set up rival churches. Donatists and Catholics intermingled freely. Catholics could become Donatists; former Donatists could become Catholic bishops. Catholic bishops could license the consecration of Donatist bishops, and promote them over Catholics.[25]

Earlier in the century, African bishops had objected to imperial policy in condemning the Three Chapters at the Fifth Ecumenical Council in Constantinople. Certain writings of Theodore of Mopsuestia, Theodoret of Cyrus, and Ibas of Edessa were condemned. As the Africans saw it, Justinian was trying to placate certain Monophysite groups, and his actions betrayed the Council of Chalcedon. The papacy followed the East and the Emperor in recognizing the validity of the Fifth Council, and calling for the condemnation of the Three Chapters. Dissent grew in Africa, and in 550, the African Church had excommunicated the Pope at the Council of Carthage. Opponents labelled the schismatics 'Donatists'; while they continued no Donatist theology, they did express the autonomy, and the rejection of outside authorities characteristic of the earlier dissenters. The imperial government put pressure on the African church to comply and was successful.

What Donatists were to Gregory is difficult to discern. Specific issues such as adherence to, or rejection of, the Three Chapters is not evident; nor is there evidence of any theological difference, although Gregory complains about their simony. Geography was a factor, for the Donatists were concentrated in Numidia, in the interior territory dominated by Berbers. Another factor was the autonomy of those labelled Donatists; their opposition to a *reichskirche* which meant their subordination to external powers. In short, these Donatists of the sixth century were less adherents to heretical beliefs than to a tradition of independence.[26] To be a Donatist was to be a rebel.

Gregory took action against the Donatists. The Catholic clergy were complacent; some even accepted bribes to tolerate Donatists (*Ep.* 2.39, 1.82). In 591, Gregory tried to reform the primate system which favoured seniority of bishops over their merit, but this was resisted by the bishops themselves (*Ep.* 1.72, 1.75). A synod was held in Numidia in 593, but instead of reform, many things were done contrary to the canons, and Gregory complained to the

[24] Duval 1991.
[25] Markus 1991.
[26] Markus 1991; Duval 1991.

exarch of Africa, Gennadius (*Ep.* 4.7 cf. *Ep.* 3.47, 3.48). Most troubling was the case of Paul, a Catholic bishop who sought the support of the Pope against alleged persecution by Donatists. However, when Gregory examined the case, he found that Paul had been condemned by his fellow bishops, and that his condemnation was supported by imperial authorities (*Ep.* 4.35). Paul's very persecution of Donatists had caused him to be condemned.

The African church ignored Gregory, and the Byzantine government wanted to keep the peace. The exarch, Gennadius, did not respond to Gregory's requests to institute a persecution of Donatists. His superior, the Praetorian Prefect Pantaleo, also refused. In 594, it appears that Gregory succeeded in getting a council at Carthage to condemn Donatists, but the imperial edict issued to suppress them was not enforced. Gregory was obliged to compromise with the African bishops on the primate system; and after a final letter of complaint to the Emperor in 596, Gregory let the matter drop. References to Donatists disappear from his letters after this date.

Dalmatia and the other churches of Illyricum

Dalmatia was a second area on the outer reaches of Rome's effective power, and the site of the most curious of Gregory's actions. Gregory received complaints of loose living against Natalis, the Bishop of Salona, made by Natalis's archdeacon, Honoratus. Angered at Honoratus, Bishop Natalis devised a fitting revenge. Honoratus was removed from his archdeaconry and forcibly ordained to the priesthood, an elevation that disqualified him from further office. Gregory was enraged at this travesty, and attempted to get Honoratus restored. When his letters were ignored by Natalis, Gregory threatened to excommunicate and depose him in a letter addressed to the suffragan bishops and the Praetorian Prefect of Illyricum (*Ep.* 2.18, 2.20). Finally, Natalis complied and wrote a witty letter defending his luxurious dinner parties as sanctioned even in the Old Testament. Gregory replied sarcastically that he would tolerate Natalis's dinner parties only if he, like Abraham, entertained angels (*Ep.* 2.44).

Ironically, this clash of personalities and values worsened on Natalis's death in 593. Who would succeed him? Gregory approved of Honoratus, but Natalis's friends (including the Byzantine government) supported Maximus, whose lax reputation made him unacceptable to Gregory. Through bribery and an imperial rescript, Maximus was installed as bishop in 594 by armed force. Opponents were ill-treated. When word reached Rome, Gregory refused to recognize Maximus, now excommunicated, and he pretended to be ignorant of the Emperor's will.

Maximus defied Gregory and continued to say mass. Gregory's letter of excommunication was posted publicly, where it was torn to shreds by a populace angered by outside interference. Maximus retaliated by accusing Gregory of contriving the death of Bishop Malchus of Dalmatia. Malchus had died in prison under mysterious circumstances after his trial in Rome for maladministration of the Roman patrimony. The brazenness of Maximus and his tenacity reveal Gregory's vulnerability. Imperial officials still sided with Maximus as the legitimate bishop, and Maurice tried to settle the affair by commanding Gregory to accept Maximus, and ordering Maximus to go to Rome.

Gregory's response followed the fine line of discretion. He would obey the Emperor and forgive Maximus his personal insults. He could not, however, overlook Maximus's other sins, and these would have to be investigated. Gregory protested, 'If the affairs of bishops committed to my care are to be settled by patronage at the court of the most serene ruler, woe is me! What use am I to the Church?' (*Ep.* 5.39). Gregory took a firm stance, staking his honour and his life (at least rhetorically).

> You know how much I can suffer, and I am prepared to die rather than allow the church of the apostle St Peter to degenerate in my time. You know my ways, that I am long-suffering, but once I have decided to forebear no longer, I face every danger with joy (*Ep.* 5.6).

Gregory had the obstinacy and valour of a martyr, at least in principle.

Four years later, in 599, the affair ended with a compromise. Maximus never came to trial, but he agreed to do public penance in Ravenna. For three hours he prostrated himself and cried out 'I have sinned against God and the blessed pope Gregory'. Then he swore an oath that he was innocent of the charges lodged against him. On a practical level, Gregory conceded more than Maximus in this whole affair, but he won points on a symbolic scale. Maximus had challenged Gregory's prestige and honour, and Gregory defended it successfully. The extremity of Gregory's rhetoric revealed the underlying limits of his power, and the extent to which Gregory could react to personal insults and differences, despite his disclaimers to put aside personal grudges (*Ep.* 6.26, 6.48). Nevertheless, the final settlement did allow Gregory to gain face: the symbolic victory of humiliating an enemy publicly was enormously important in Gregory's cultural milieu.

Dealings with other churches of Illyricum reveal both the ambitious extension of Gregory's authority and its attenuation at such a distance. The emperor gained by default. The two most important sees subject to the papacy were those of Thessalonica and Prima Justiniana, both of whose bishops were apostolic vicars. Charges of misconduct by Adrian, the Bishop of Thebes, were brought to the emperor, who in turn ordered trial by the Bishop of Larissa, despite Thebes's exemption from Larissa's jurisdiction (*Ep.* 3.6, 3.7). The condemned Bishop of Thebes appealed to the emperor for justice,

and the emperor in turn ordered Gregory's *responsalis* and a chancellor to
make an inquiry. Before this took place, a confession was extorted from the
accused Bishop Adrian. The emperor again made the decisions, this time
ordering that Bishop John of Prima Justiniana should try the case. In the trial,
many illegalities took place and Bishop Adrian was again degraded from
office. Only then did Bishop Adrian of Thebes appeal to Rome. And when
Gregory summoned the accusers, no one came. Gregory decided the matter
by reading written records, and reproved both the Bishop of Larissa for usurp-
ing jurisdiction, and the Bishop of Prima Justiniana for violating the canons
in his trial of Adrian. Adrian was eventually rehabilitated. No one resisted
Gregory's authority here, but Gregory was called in only as a last resort. The
emperor was the more central player.

The emperor's actual power and Gregory's moral authority clashed over
plans for the emperor to depose the Bishop of Prima Justiniana due to ill-
health (*Ep*. 11.29). Gregory argued either that the bishop must be allowed to
resign, or a coadjutor should be appointed. But he conceded the emperor's
power to do what he would. With careful discretion, he negotiated a position that recognized the authority of both pope and emperor. 'If what he [i.e.,
the emperor] does is in accordance with the canons, we conform to it; if it
is not, we submit to it, as far as we can do so without sin' (*Ep*. 11.29; cf.
Ep. 13.6). Such discreet formulations appeared when Gregory was forced by
contradictory commands, both to obey the emperor as God's representative,
and yet to obey God's law as pope.

One of the most bitter disagreements between the emperor and the pope
came over the emperor's interference in a jurisdictional dispute with the
Bishop of Corfu. Gregory considered the emperor's decision illegal, wrong,
unjust and uncanonical. Nevertheless, he did not publish his own opinion, 'lest
[he] should appear to be acting contrary to the commands of my gracious
lord the emperor, or in contempt of him – God forbid!' (*Ep*. 14.8). Working
behind the scenes, Gregory was able to arrange a compromise.

Istria

Closer to home, Istria remained schismatic over the Three Chapters. Gregory
made little progress in resolving the conflict, indeed his efforts must have
caused frustration and anguish. Like the Donatists in the mid-sixth century,
the Istrians did not consider the condemned writings of Theodore of
Mopsuestia, Theodoret of Cyrus and Ibas of Edessa to be heretical. They rejected the Fifth Ecumenical Council as abrogating the Council of Chalcedon.
This rejection asserted the independence and autonomy of the Istrians, for it
separated them from the emperor, who supported the Fifth Ecumenical Council, and from the papacy, which supported the emperor.

Gregory took a firm stand the first year of his pontificate, sending troops under the command of a tribune and an imperial guardsmen to the Patriarch of Aquileia, Severus. The troops delivered a rebuke of the Istrians' apostasy, and summoned Severus and his adherents to a synod at St Peter's (*Ep*. 1.16). The Istrians responded by appealing to the emperor. They asserted their orthodoxy, and threatened to ally with neighbouring bishops in Gaul, if they were not left alone. The emperor wanted to avoid the political consequences of such an alliance, so he ordered Gregory to desist. Gregory complied, although he suspected that the Istrians had blackmailed and bribed the emperor to act against the true interests of the Church, and indeed, the empire. Ironically, Gregory got a measure of justice, but at the expense of charity. A year later when a fire swept Aquileia, Gregory refused to send relief to the 'enemies' of the Church (*Ep*. 2.38).

The prestige of Rome gradually won over some of the schismatics, and Gregory did all he could to persuade schismatics and support those returning, even giving them land to which they were not entitled. The submission to imperial authority must have grieved Gregory's conscience, because as pastor, he bore responsibility for the souls of the innocent bystanders involved. He wrote to John of Ravenna that he did not cease to write to the emperor 'in zeal and ardor' about the matter (*Ep*. 2.45). That he never gave up the hope of force is evidenced by his call for repression of the schismatics again after Maurice's death (*Ep*. 13.34). The Istrian schismatics, like the Donatists in Africa aroused Gregory's most vehement and righteous anger. Heresy and schism were works of the devil, and foreshadowings of the Antichrist. One only erred in being merciful to such evil. The only right action was to excise the cancer that threatened to destroy the integrity of the Church's body. No choices existed here. Tolerance was 'softness' and 'laxity' toward evil – itself an evil.

Greater Italy

The disruptions of Justinian's reconquest and the Lombard invasions meant the consolidation of as many as 42 episcopal sees. Lucania and Apulia were particularly dislocated, as were coastal and frontier towns.[27] The Picene area had to be rebuilt completely. The difficulties Gregory faced in his efforts to rebuild the Church's hierarchy are evidenced by a peculiar violation of his own rules against the ordination of laymen. In Aprutina, a laymen aptly named Oportunus was tonsured and ordained as bishop in 601 (*Ep*. 12.4).

Areas that were not as devastated posed their own problems. The sees of Milan, Ravenna and Aquileia had their own degrees of autonomy; and even

---

[27] Richards 1980, 100–4; Brown 1984, 40.

bishops in Sicily could cause problems. Gregory's relations with the see of Milan reveal quiet and effective tenacity on the part of the bishop of Milan. The bishop had a tradition of independence from Rome, and controlled the diocese of Italia Annonaria with the imperial capital of Ravenna, whose bishop was under his jurisdiction. However, the Lombard invasions had effectively limited his power base to the coastal region of Liguria, where he lived in Genoa with his clergy. Gregory asserted his right to confirm the election of the Bishop of Milan in refusing to accept Constantius until he knew whether he was acceptable to the clergy exiled in Genoa. When Constantius ended up in a lawsuit with a soldier, Fortunatus, who appealed to Gregory for help, Gregory stood firm in wanting to try the case in Rome (*Ep.* 4.37). When Constantius died, Gregory succeeded in backing the choice of Deusdedit against Agilulf's choice for the post.

With the see of Milan weakened, Roman authority was enhanced. In 578, a Roman cleric, John, became Bishop of Ravenna. Gregory had a good rapport with John, dedicated his *Regula pastoralis liber* to John in 591, and praised him for his position against Istrian schismatics. However, Ravenna was the centre of imperial authority, and even the bishop had pretensions to glory of his own. He would assert the custom of wearing the pallium; he would allow his clergy the status symbols of special saddle cloths (*mappulae)* and this would pique Gregory.

The late sixth century is characterized by the use of elaborate regalia, a proliferation of titles, frequent ceremonies and processions before impressionable audiences, privileged behaviors alloted to certain statuses, etc. Gregory's hatred of pride and hypocrisy stemmed from a deep struggle to define and foster legitimate authority when the very ground of the authority was uncertain and unstable. Surely, authority and prestige were better than naked coercion, but *how* could one secure such honours? Did the morally right means suffice to achieve the desired end? The obsession with the minutiae of distinction was proportional to the fragility of its validation, to the dissonance that often existed between external status and internal merit. 'Do not be concerned with what you have, but what you are', Gregory preached (*HEv.* 2.28.3) 'God will judge not the prerogative of rank, but by the merits of our works', Gregory assured the bishops of Numidia (*Ep.* 1.75). In the purity of the Church, status and honour were supposed to be an accurate reflection of merit, but Gregory recognized this was not always the case.

Pride was the great sin of those who violated the right order of the Church. Gregory rebuked the pride of the Archbishop of Ravenna 'with honey and venom' when the archbishop presumed to wear the pallium not merely during the mass, but during solemn processions through the city, and even in audiences with the laity. His clergy also usurped a privilege possessed by the Roman clergy alone, that of using *mappulae* in processions (*Ep.* 3.54, 3.67;

Append. 6). The outcome was more a victory for the archbishop than for Gregory. Romanus, the exarch of Ravenna, and George, the Praetorian Prefect of Italy, pressured Gregory to respect the privileges of Ravenna. Gregory conceded the use of *mappulae*, and compromised on the use of the pallium. When John died in 595, Gregory managed to block the imperial candidate and get his old friend and fellow monk Marinianus elected to the see. But even friendship with Gregory could not dampen the enthusiasm for display, and the question of the pallium arose again. Gregory called for an investigation of historical usage, but never succeeded in convening a council. Marinianus was little better than John and it must have been painful to bear such a disappointment from a friend. Gregory would continue to write kindly and solicitous letters to Marinianus until his death (*Ep.* 13.26; 13.30).

Constantinople and the eastern churches

The political roots of Gregory's dispute with the Patriarch of Constantinople over the use of the title 'Ecumenical Patriarch' are deep and complicated. But Gregory's reaction was dramatic. Whatever the mysterious origins, the Patriarch's action became symbolic of a whole system of values, institutions and behaviours that Gregory found disastrous. The dispute is less a political incident than a cultural war in which Gregory's deepest ideals and anxieties were manifest.

John the Faster, Patriarch of Constantinople, allowed himself to be called 'Ecumenical Patriarch' (or 'Universal Bishop') at a synod in Constantinople in 588. The title had been used by patriarchs at the synod of Constantinople in 518, and even earlier applied to Pope Leo at Chalcedon. But John was the first to apply it to himself, excluding others. Pope Pelagius protested, and nullified the synod.

Gregory repeated Pelagius' protests, only to be commanded by Emperor Maurice to desist. When two Eastern presbyters appealed to Rome, Gregory was able to assert jurisdiction over Constantinople. But this did not mean that John dropped his title. Gregory wrote more letters to Constantinople condemning John's hypocrisy and pride, and it is evident that the issue grew to represent a threat to Gregory's spiritual and moral value system. Gregory admonished John to love humility, and not abase others by raising himself. He accused John of imitating Lucifer, and reminded him of the Last Judgement, when John would be held accountable for the sinful title he tried to use to subject [Christ's] members to himself (*Ep.* 5.44). To Constantina, Gregory wrote vividly of John's pride and the implication of this for world order: 'By this pride of his what else is signified than that the times of the Antichrist are already at hand?' (*Ep.* 5.39). The most desperate arguments were reserved for Maurice. 'The peace of the republic depends on the peace of the universal church', Gregory wrote (*Ep.* 5.37), and the Lord had assuredly placed his church in the hands of Peter. Barbarians had invaded, and the empire lay in ruins as God's punishment for [their] sins. And priests, who should be weeping in dust and ashes, instead sought 'names of vanity and glory in new and profane titles'. Gregory threatened, 'every one that exalteth himself shall be humbled'.[28] Those who would not obey the canons must be coerced by the commands of the emperor; John must be restrained from injuring the Church. Gregory also wrote to the Patriarchs of Alexandria and Antioch for their support.

Schism was averted by John's death, and the emperor's actions. In 596, he appointed Cyriacus, an amiable man, to be Patriarch of Constantinople and ordered Gregory to receive him with kindness and make no further trouble about 'an idle name'. Gregory received Cyriacus himself with charity, but protested he could not consent to remain silent to sin: 'when Antichrist comes and calls himself God, will not that be very idle, yet extremely wicked?' (*Ep.* 7.30). Cyriacus continued to use the offensive title, but Gregory's protests were ignored and the patriarch appears to have gained authority. In 599, a synod was called in Constantinople, inviting bishops under Gregory's jurisdiction, from eastern Illyricum. Gregory wrote to his bishops reminding them that the synod was invalid without the authority and consent of the Holy See, and he threatened to excommunicate them if they countenanced the title of 'Ecumenical Patriarch' (*Ep.* 9.156). It appears Gregory was ignored.

Gregory's final hope came when the Emperor Maurice died. Phocas issued a decree that the 'Apostolic See of St Peter, that is the Roman Church, should be the head of all churches'. Phocas was shifting his base of power to the Roman West and the papacy, suspicious actions to those in the East. Phocas's recognition of Gregory still did not stop the patriarch's use of the title, and Gregory died without getting Cyriacus to yield. Ironically, later Roman popes decided the best strategy was cooption, and they began to style themselves as ecumenical bishops and ecumenical popes using the very title Gregory had despised.

Politics aside, the dispute over title raised issues fundamental to Gregory's definition of spiritual life and proper behaviour. Gregory would say both that injustice must be suffered, and that one must prevent injustice (cf. *Mor.* 31.13.22). Humility and discretion were paradoxical ways to rule. As 'servant of the servants of God', Gregory was never to compromise the paradox of the honoured man who condescended willingly to a humble status, even as the Logos deigned to become incarnate and suffer as a man. But Gregory's epithet must be matched with his response to the claim of John of Constantinople, to be 'Ecumenical Patriarch'. Gregory cited Matthew 20:27, 'who-

[28] Luke 14:11; 18:14.

ever will be chief among you shall be the least of all' (*Ep.* 5.44), and noted that the devil claimed to 'be like the Most High'.[29] Lines were drawn unmistakably; correct behaviour was indisputably prescribed. With Gregory, the inversion of humility was so formalized that it became its own form of honour. 'Do not desire to *seem* more than you are, so you may be able to be *more* than you seem' (*Ep.* 5.15). 'It is the usual mark of the Elect', Gregory said, 'That they always think less of themselves than they really are' (*Mor.* 34.22.44). Humility could become formalized, a ritual to preserve proper order. 'In the thought of the heart I should prefer [another] to myself, and he in return should prefer me to himself' (*Mor.* 34.22.43). By such discreet courtesies the community could be kept in equilibrium: 'When the heart is kept down on either side no one may be elated by the honour bestowed on him', Gregory argued (*Mor.* 34.22.43).

Gregory's extraordinary anger at John of Constantinople's assumption of the title 'Ecumenical Patriarch' was rooted in this distinction between true virtue, discretion and hypocrisy which was fundamental to Gregory's world view. His highly emotional response seems wildly disproportionate to John's actions. A complicated misunderstanding lay at the heart of the controversy.[30] When John used the title, he was following Byzantine tradition. To say he was 'Ecumenical Patriarch' meant that he followed doctrine as defined by the emperor. It was a way of assuring the world that the patriarch stood for orthodoxy from the perspective of the universality of the Christian empire – the Church as supported by the secular authorities. The title had also been applied to Leo, who interpreted imperial orthodoxy for East and West at Chalcedon. In Justinian's era, the title had an official character, and after the Fifth Ecumenical Council in 553, the title referred especially to the Patriarch of Constantinople who had the duty of formulating imperial doctrine to avoid the heretical extremes of monophysitism and ditheism.

Gregory did not understand that the patriarch used the term 'universal' to express the doctrine common to eastern and western Christians according to imperial law. As Gregory saw it, those who had used the title had been at odds with Rome, and their orthodoxy was suspect. The papacy could not accept the title when it was in disagreement with the dogmatic positions of the patriarch. The title was used at the synod of Constantinople in 587, in the restoration of Gregory of Antioch. Pelagius II had protested against the title and the judgement. In 595, Gregory discovered that the title was used for the Patriarch, who presided at a trial condemning two priests as heretical. Gregory rejected this condemnation, and the title of authority claimed by the judge. Gregory wrote to Maurice that the title should not be used, as

[29] Isaiah 14:14.
[30] Tuilier 1986.

some of the previous patriarchs such as Nestorius and Macedonius had been heretics. To follow them would be to lead the Church to schism. In Gregory's eyes, the Patriarch of Constantinople and the Eastern bishops could not be trusted to define orthodoxy. The East favoured the reconciliation of heretics and supported Eulogus in promoting the Alexandrian formula, *mia physis tou theou logou sesarkomene*. The West could not agree to this, for they held resolutely to the Christology of Leo.

While principally dogmatic differences separated East and West, other points of conflict existed. The eastern church favoured the Greens, with their Monophysite sympathies. This circus faction drew its support from urban populations of mercantile aristocrats and artisans. Rome, in contrast, favoured the Blues, the party of the Roman aristocracy. The elevation of Constantinople would have threatened political equilibrium. Rome needed the political and military support of the Byzantine government, both for civil and ecclesiastical policy. A decline in the prestige of Rome would make it all the easier for the emperor to ignore Gregory's pleas for assistance.

The patriarch of the capital city sought to make the see of Constantinople supreme in the eastern empire, thereby setting up Constantinople in rivalry with Rome in an implicitly divided empire. Rome would be the loser on all counts. The unity of the Church would be shattered. Rome would be cut off from the more important sees, and left to face an increasingly barbarian church with a whole new set of problems. When historical implications of this controversy are considered, the depth of Gregory's response is no longer surprising.

The dispute over the title became a dispute about Roman primacy to later generations. While Gregory believed in the equality of churches and bishops, he also believed in the primacy of Rome as the heir of St Peter, divinely appointed. Rome was 'head of all the churches', whose authority was necessary to ratify councils, and whose bishop was empowered to discipline others and govern the Church. Gregory despised John's claim, not just because it threatened Rome's authority, but because the kind of authority John and Cyriacus claimed was extremely dangerous and divisive. Worldly and unchristian in its conception, it elevated itself at the expense of others. Why could not Rome be accused of the same? When the Patriarch of Antioch called Gregory 'Ecumenical Patriarch', Gregory was offended at the 'proud title'. It offended equity. 'In position you are my brother, in character you are my father' (*Ep.* 8.29). Gregory conceived of power and authority in a way quite different from the easterners. Power was dangerous precisely because it freed one from self-restraint and from obedience to others. One could only undertake office with an internal disposition of continuous penitence. An office meant sacrifice, service and obedience to the needs of others. Gregory's own title, 'servus servorum dei', meant that the only safe power lay in obedience;

in the abnegation of power to dominate and the acceptance of the burden to serve.

IV. Relations with secular authorities

Byzantine rulers

Gregory was ready to call on secular powers to advance the aims of the Church. 'For the more powerful [the prince] is toward the world, the more does he prevail for the Creator of the world', Gregory wrote (*Mor.* 31.6.8). Gregory accepted the power of secular leaders in the service of the Church, just as he acknowledged the Church's own prosperity in the world. Secular powers were a part of the concord of the Church. Members had complementary abilities and differences, each supplied what the other lacked: the 'eyes' of the more spiritual members proffered spiritual guidance to those less able to see truths, while the humble 'feet' laboured in the 'dust' of the world, protecting the delicate eyes. Their interdependence insured the humility of each (*Mor.* 31.13.25).

Nevertheless, Gregory fully recognized the dangerous carnal power possessed by secular authorities. The secular prince was the fearsome rhinoceros of Job,[31] swollen with a horn of pride. He had terrified the weak, and wrought destruction in his unregenerate selfishness (*Mor.* 31.1ff). But once tempered and bound by conversion, the prince could be harnessed to plough the Lord's field. He was bound and had his own *ministerium*, his duty of serving the Church: to repress heresy, destroy the Church's enemies, chasten the wicked and protect the weak. Church and state had complementary needs and obligations. The Church needed to remember that only the power of the Lord 'inclined the powers which He had conferred on an earthly prince for a temporal purpose, for the labour of his reverence' (*Mor.* 31.6.8). The Church had its duties: to pray for the welfare of princes and the defeat of their enemies (*Ep.* 3.61, 5.30, 7.5, 7.7). In turn, the secular prince needed to recognize that he owed servile obedience to the Author of his power, and he was obliged to honour the Church entrusted to his protection (*Mor.* 31.6.8–10; cf. *Ep.* 5.39, 5.36, 7.6, 9.154).[32] Since the peace of the republic depended upon the peace of the Church (*Ep.* 5.37), the shrewd ruler ought to realize that his own interests were allied and continuous with those of the Church. The earthly kingdom could indeed serve the heavenly kingdom (*Ep.* 3.61).

Gregory had a firm conviction of the responsibilities secular powers owed to the Church, and an equally strong sense of his own duty to obey secular

---

[31] Job 39: 9–12.
[32] Straw 1991.

powers as ordained by God (cf. *Reg. past.* 3.4). Subjects got the rulers they deserved, although one could not always penetrate God's mysterious purposes in alloting rulers. He might ordain righteous rulers for the advancement of his people, or permit wicked rulers to rage for the discipline and chastisement of his flock. Gregory felt that Agilulf was such a punishment for his personal sins; so, too, the complacency or the hostility of the Emperor Maurice to Gregory's goals were chastisements of Gregory's own faults.

We have seen above the tension between Gregory's aims and the Emperor Maurice's policies. Maurice not only failed to offer meaningful assistance against the Lombards, but he rebuked Gregory and called him foolish for attempting to secure his own peace treaty with Agilulf. Maurice rejected Gregory's call for a persecution of Donatists in Africa, and he ordered Gregory to cease harassing Istrian schismatics. He took the opposing side in the dispute regarding the see of Salona. Relations between Maurice and Gregory had soured early in Gregory's pontificate, and the dispute set the pattern for Gregory's behaviour toward the emperor. In 593, Maurice issued an edict prohibiting those who were under obligations to the state (i.e., soldiers, *curiales*, officials, etc.) from becoming monks or clerics. Gregory was furious. He could accept their exclusion from the clergy, for such really only traded one type of secular career for another. But to forbid them from becoming monks was to threaten the very salvation of those who could achieve virtue by no other way than seclusion.

Gregory acted with characteristic, if puzzling, discretion. On one hand, he protested vehemently and, on the other, he submitted to the emperor's law and promulgated the emperor's edict. 'I have thus done my duty on both sides. I have obeyed the emperor, and yet have not kept back what I felt ought to be said on behalf of God' (*Ep.* 3.61). A compromise was later reached.

In subsequent conflicts, Gregory exercised discretion in similar ways. He would forgive the insults Maximus of Salona had levelled against him, but he could not overlook his sins against God, which rendered him excommunicate. While he considered an imperial decree regarding the jurisdiction of the Bishop of Corfu illegal, he nevertheless refrained from publishing his own decision lest he appear to have contempt for the emperor. The loyal subject must be like David, obedient to Saul as the Lord's anointed. And like David, he could register his differences in the Lord's sight, for just as David cut the hem of Saul's cloak when none were looking, so the subject could disagree discreetly and rebuke the ruler (*Reg. past.* 3.4).

Such treatment of the emperor as the Lord's anointed was structured in ambivalences. One could call for aid, but one needed to be self-sufficient. One rightly reminded the ruler of duties, but one needed to adjust to him and recognize his weaknesses. Ultimately, one had to obey laws, but one was also obliged to rebuke his wrongs in order to discharge one's own duty and free oneself from culpability. Rebuke protected God's servants: the Ethiopian went into the bath black and emerged black, but the keeper still received his pay (*Ep.* 3.62). The ruler was always the rhinoceros – dangerous, though harnessed. He was God's chosen, but either for good or for evil.

Appreciating this ambivalence, Gregory's letters to Phocas should not come as a shock. Phocas came to power in 602, after assassinating Maurice and seizing power. Gregory wrote to the usurper and assassin letters of joyful congratulation and blessing, because Maurice had been such a scourge: 'Sometimes, when the sins of man are to be punished, one man is raised up, by whose severity the necks of the people are bowed beneath the yoke of tribulation'. Gregory now hoped for an end to evils: 'May all enjoy the peaceful possession of their own property ... may each regain the liberty which is his due' (*Ep.* 13.32). Phocas did recognize the see of St Peter as the head of Christian churches.

Western monarchs

Rulers were to serve the Church and advance its aims; they could be used profitably by the Church, without reticence or apology. However, most of Gregory's attempts to woo the Franks and the English met with little more success than his efforts with Maurice. The resolution of the chief problems in the Frankish realm – simony, the ordination of laymen, Arianism, the Three Chapters, schism, paganism – needed the vigorous cooperation of Frankish rulers. Gregory wrote complimentary letters to Brunhilda and King Childebert commending their loyalty to the Catholic faith (*Ep.* 6.5, 6.6). His letters to Brunhilda may seem especially unsettling, but her violence (while obviously reprehensible) was no worse than that of other Frankish monarchs. Such power could be useful, for it was the rulers' duty to protect the Church with whatever powers they possessed, to extend its boundaries as they extended their own, to defeat its enemies as they defeated their own (cf. *Ep.* 1.72, 1.73, 2.20, 6.7). To Brunhilda, Gregory stressed the mutual advantage of a right relationship with God: 'Do what is God's and He will do yours' (*Ep.* 11.49). Gregory went as far as imagining that rulers had roles complementary to that of priests making offerings to God: Brunhilda offered a sacrifice of expiation in purging her clergy of immoral practice (*Ep.* 11.46); she offered another in repressing simony (*Ep.* 11.49). Ethelbert offered a sacrifice in the conversion of his people (*Ep.* 11.35). But whether such complimentary language worked is not always evident.

The withholding or granting of the pallium could be a useful means of insuring a modicum of obedience. In 595, Gregory sent admonitions with his grant of the pallium and a papal vicarate to Bishop Virgilius of Arles. Gregory exhorted Virgilius never to seek his own gain, but to seek what is Christ's.

Specifically, Virgilius was to persuade King Childebert to expunge the stain of simony from his kingdom, and to prohibit the ordination of untried laymen as priests (*Ep.* 5.58). The vicarate elevated the Bishop of Arles over other bishops in the kingdom of Childebert.

At Brunhilda's request, Gregory gave the pallium to the Bishop of Autun, Syagrius, but not before Gregory had extracted a promise that Syagrius hold a synod against simony and other abuses (*Ep.* 9.223). Gregory wrote to Brunhilda, Kings Theoderic and Theodobert, and the bishops of Autun, Arles, and Vienne seeking their support for the synod (*Ep.* 9.214, 9.216). Gregory sent special encouragement to the Bishop of Gap, who had visited Rome. Gregory now awarded him the use of dalmatics and requested that he attend the synod (*Ep.* 9.220). Despite his careful work, the Franks ignored Gregory. However, Gregory persisted. Two years later, in 601, Gregory wrote to Brunhilda and other Frankish kings (Theoderic, Theodebert and Clothaire), urging them again to convene such a synod (*Ep.* 11.48, 11.47, 11.50, 11.51). While councils were held in 601 and again in 603–4, they did not succeed in curbing the abuses of simony, lay appointments and other vices, for these practices were an intrinsic part of the kinship and patronage systems that held Frankish society together.

Gregory did not intervene directly in the Gallic church by writing to bishops and priests suspected of simony.[33] Instead, he recognized the authority of the monarch in episcopal elections, and the crucial role the episcopacy had to play in the reform of the Church. In short, the Gallic church had an autonomy: its own hierarchy of bishops, its own councils, organization and liturgy. Gregory might criticize the practice of the kings, but he never questioned their rights to approve elections. Here Gregory's political theology worked against the formation of a unified, hierarchical church. Kings and queens were God's servants, for better or worse. The tenuous relationship established between the papacy and Frankish royalty was not continued after Gregory's death. The Frankish church continued to develop its own character.

Several of Gregory's letters to the Franks commend Augustine to their protection. Without this, Augustine's mission to convert the English might well have been impossible. In 596, Augustine set out but returned after reaching Aix. Gregory insisted that they begin again. King Ethelbert was converted and probably baptized in 597, and all of Kent became Christian. Augustine's success was such that reinforcements came in 601, and Augustine received the pallium with archiepiscopal jurisdiction. A second see was to be created in York. Gregory believed a single church could be created in England, with metropolitan bishops at London and York who had received

---

[33] Pietri 1991.

the pallium from Rome. These bishops were to have jurisdiction over Celtic British churches.[34]

Gregory's *Responsa* to Augustine preserved in Bede (*MGH, Ep.* 11.56a) is considered authentic.[35] In it, Gregory outlined a characteristically pragmatic programme for dealing with new Christians. Augustine could select whatever rites and customs seemed best, either Gallican or Roman, 'For we ought not to value things on account of places, but places on account of things'. Theft in churches should be punished according to the motivation of the thief, be it hunger or greed. New converts were subject to stringent incest restrictions to marriage; the old were left alone. Still the Roman mission faltered when it encountered Christians converted years earlier in southern Wales who would not give up their own tribal traditions. Augustine's attitude further alienated the Celtic clergy. While Augustine did not succeed in uniting with the Celtic churches, he did establish a foundation for the English church. Gregory's vision of a Church reaching even 'the extremities of the earth' (*Mor.* 27.11.21) grew closer to realization.

The Visigoths in Spain were converted to Catholicism from Arianism at the Third Council of Toledo in 589, just before the beginning of Gregory's pontificate.[36] King Reccared saw the value of unifying his kingdom with a common faith, and upon his conversion began a campaign of suppressing Arianism – burning books, banning Arians from office and destroying the church organization. These harsh measures brought about a quick transformation. Gregory's friend Leander of Seville played a leading role at the Council of Toledo, and Gregory asked Leander to keep watch on Reccared. Beyond that, Rome had no role in the conversion of Spain. Indeed, Gregory was so pleased by Reccared's works that he wondered if he should appear before God at the Last Judgement empty, while Reccared would bring with him many flocks of faithful ones (*Ep.* 9.229). Here the 'preaching' of the ruler had been more effective than the preaching of the priest.

V. Conclusions

The opinions of the contemporaries

Gregory is known to us from the writings of a contemporary, Gregory of Tours, in his *Historia Francorum* and from the *Liber pontificalis*. Isidore of Seville gives two short notices of Gregory (*de vir. illustr.* 27) dating from the first half of the seventh century, and Ildefonsus of Toledo gives a reference to Gregory in his own *De vir. illustr.* (1) from the second half of the

[34] Chadwick 1991.
[35] Meyvaert 1986.
[36] Vilella 1991.

same century. An anonymous monk of Whitby wrote the first *Life of Gregory*, probably in about 713; and around 731, Bede published some letters of Gregory in his *Ecclesiastical History* 2.1. The English preserved the memory of Gregory as the pope who was responsible for sending Augustine of Canterbury for their conversion. When Pope John VIII (872–82) became aware of this tradition, he commissioned John the Deacon to write a life of Gregory. The other major early life was written by Paul the Deacon, dating from between 770 and 780. His *Historia Langobardorum* is also important for knowledge of Gregory's circumstances. Compilations were made of Gregory's writings by his secretary Paterius, the *Liber testimoniorum* (*PL* 79, 685–1136). Of the compilations of Gregory's works made by Taio of Saragossa in the mid-seventh century, part of one survives on the Old and New Testament (*PL* Suppl. 4, 263–419). His *sententiarum libri V* are arranged topically and draw heavily on Paterius (*PL* 80, 727–990). Lathcen (d. 661) also made an important compilation of Gregory's works in his *elogia*. Various other compilations and florilegia were made of the *Moralia* in the Middle Ages.[37]

Of these medieval witnesses to Gregory's life and works, two give accounts of his final days and the reactions to his death. Gregory died on March 12, 604 (September 3rd is his feast day). He was buried in the portico of the Basilica of St Peter, in front of the sacristy. John the Deacon records a 16-line epitaph which refers to Gregory as 'Consul of God' (Io. Diac. *vita Greg.* 4.68). When Gregory died, the brief peace with the Lombards was ending, and a famine had again struck the city. The succeeding pope, Sabinian, was Gregory's former apocrisiarius in Constantinople and a partisan of the clerical party opposed to Gregory. Sabinian withdrew the grain dole. In Paul's account, Sabinian expressly reversed Gregory's policy and was rebuked by a vision of Gregory. John writes that certain parties spread rumours that Gregory had bankrupted the Church, and the fury of the people was such that they stormed the Lateran to burn his books. Peter the Deacon checked them by recounting the miracle that was to provide the main symbol in Gregory's iconography. Peter had often seen the Holy Spirit in the shape of a dove inspiring the Pope. Because of this story, Gregory is generally portrayed with a dove.

An assessment

Gregory's significance lies both in his activities as a writer and as pope. Despite his popularity in the Middle Ages and the Counter Reformation, the modern era has neglected Gregory. Estimation of him reached a low point with Adolf Harnack in the nineteenth century, who believed that Gregory created a crude work-religion (*ergismus*) appealing to a declining civilization

---

[37] Wasselynck 1952–69; Matter 1994.

sunk in superstition and magic. As a writer, Gregory is typically but wrongly compared with Augustine, or his theology is mistakenly systematized into scholastic categories. In part, this is because Gregory is a 'hinge' figure joining past and future, east and west. Gregory's debt to Cassian and the monastic tradition of the desert is substantial. He also studied Ambrose, and encountered the latter's Neoplatonism. Gregory had some knowledge of Origen and Gregory Nazianzen, as well as strong empathy for Tertullian's harsh views about the body, soul, and the value of suffering. Gregory will read Augustine through a lens of asceticism, softening Augustine's attitudes toward free will and grace with more optimistic attitudes coming from the East. With Gregory, the ascetic ideals of desert monasticism became more flexible, and now applicable to the Christian community as a whole. Gregory adapted Augustine's thought to the wider and less sophisticated audience of the Middle Ages, preserving much by allowing subtle changes of emphasis. While most points of Augustine's theology remained, Gregory tempered Augustine's harsher positions on grace and free will, creating a theology at once practical, possible and intellectually satisfying.

In moral theology, Gregory was deeply influenced by Stoicism. He refined ideals of self-discipline and created a new Christian synthesis. His was a spirituality for adversity, adapted to the challenges of troubled times. His themes were universal and timeless: the mystery of suffering; the failure of virtue despite one's will; the conflict between contemplative withdrawal and active service. Pragmatic and realistic, Gregory was the moral theologian who gave answers to life's problems; he was the preacher who instructed disciples in clear principles of right behavior. This is not to say that he did not appreciate the mysteries of God's ways. But Gregory was most interested in how visible signs could serve as mediating links to invisible realities, how a saint could tame a bear, or a demon appear disguised as a bath attendant. Gregory did not dispel the mysteriousness of God's order in the world, why the good so often suffer while the wicked succeed. Instead, he systematized this mystery, delineating how either adversity or prosperity could precede either election or damnation. Knowing this, one could meet the fundamental challenge of life's alternations of fortune only with a disposition of continuous penitence. Like humility, penitence was central in Gregory's thought, and his emphasis on penitence anticipates the growing importance of the sacraments, and the increasing role of the Church as an institution securing the salvation of the individual soul. This is the medieval world, and the centrality of the Eucharist for Gregory came to be appreciated again in the Counter Reformation.

As important as penitence was Gregory's compassion: his desire for perfection was balanced by his understanding of human limitations. Every Christian had a place in the concord of Gregory's church, from virtuous contemplatives to ordinary laity. All had imposed upon them the same command to make their lives sacrifices to God, though each sacrifice would be expressed according to individual abilities, be it in solitary contemplative silence or the busy world of charity and service to neighbour. This realism again pointed toward the future and made way for the acceptance of realms and peoples far beyond that imagined by the first Christians. In the broadest sense, Gregory's was a missionary religion in its flexibility, adaptability and understanding of fundamental human problems. Discretion served him well.

As pope, Gregory's rule was pivotal, and that same quality of careful discernment that shaped his thought also guided his actions. With the Church in disarray from the Lombard invasions and various abuses by clergy and laity alike, Gregory sought to establish effective order. He set an ideal of monastic restraint and rectitude for the administration of the Church, and rebuked consistently those who did not meet standards of rectitude. That he was not always successful in realizing his high aims is understandable, considering the complexities he faced. The autonomy and power of other churches made them quite capable of ignoring Rome. Gregory could also be very harsh. Schismatics and heretics felt the brunt of this severity. For Gregory, they were unquestionable evils, signs of the approaching Antichrist. And Gregory had no patience for the devil. Yet Gregory could be flexible. He knew when it was appropriate to change policy about idols in Anglo-Saxon England. His instructions to Augustine of Canterbury on the conversion of the English show a similar moderation. He could appreciate the need an illiterate audience would have for pictures and painting. And, as the *Regula pastoralis liber* demonstrates, Gregory thought the whole principle of effective preaching was based on designing one's message and approach to fit the specific, idiosyncratic needs of the listener.

Another aspect of Gregory's discernment appears in his administration of the papal patrimony and the Church itself. In managing the patrimony, his sheer organizational ability is impressive. He made the system work: his representatives were responsible, and they sought to extend effective control over their areas. This was a great challenge. The usurpations of both laymen and clergy were difficult to undo, but Gregory made progress. Gregory's administrative acumen was complemented with a meticulous concern for justice and a genuine determination to help the poor. Some, of course, did not benefit. While it is true Gregory used land and tax incentives to promote the conversion of pagans and Jews, he can be freed of responsibility for more odious policies of the forced conversion of subjects on Church lands.

The prosperity Gregory fostered from this patrimony made possible the provision and defence of Rome during the years of the Lombard aggression and imperial weakness. With discretion and flexibility, Gregory adjusted to his situation and took action. The papacy assumed many of the duties of the secular government, even though this engaged the Church in dangerous secular affairs.

He organized defences for Rome and the south, and at times he conducted a foreign policy separate from that of the Byzantine government. Gregory undertook welfare programmes and performed civic responsibilities once carried out by the Roman authorities. By default, the Roman papacy came to dominate the politics and society of Rome. In this sense, Rome's experience was not different from many late antique and early medieval cities which came to rely on their bishops for temporal as well as spiritual welfare. These bishops dominated their own areas and had their own ambitions and claims. Only over time, were the bishops of Rome able to make use of the historical advantages the ancient capital possessed to surpass rival cities and bishops.

Gregory often felt frustrated by the Byzantine government, whether because of its policy in the Lombard wars, or its actions with regard to the Church. The Byzantine government had its own agenda of keeping the empire stable. Wisely, the government ignored Gregory's call for the persecution of the Donatists. The emperor also told him to refrain from pursuing Istrian schimatics. Imperial power overshadowed papal authority in the affairs of the Illyrian churches; and the emperor even presumed to make pastoral decisions, restricting those who wished to enter the service of God. Gregory could protest, doing his duty to God. But he also chose to obey imperial policy, as he had a duty to obey the emperor as well. Gregory's attitude toward the Byzantine government always betrayed that ambivalence. A felicitous martyrdom was not to be had by opposing imperial authorities. The emperor was God's appointed, for better or worse. Perhaps it was predictable that the Byzantine government did not side with Gregory in the dispute over the title of 'Ecumenical Patriarch'. The emperor and the pope scarcely ever saw things the same way. The emperor tried to calm Gregory and minimize the importance of the controversy. Gregory's rhetoric grew strident as he saw the apocalypse foretold in the event.

Gregory weighed all actions *sub specie aeternitatis*. Had he done his duty? How would he be judged? He must advance God's ways in the world, and this meant carrying God's word to the heathen. Gregory hoped to expand the Church not only by converting pagans and Jews in the Mediterranean countryside, but also by reaching into the areas inhabited by Germanic tribes. Gregory hoped the Lombards would be converted from Arianism. He wrote to Reccared and Leander of Seville, encouraging the new Catholicism of Spain. He cultivated the leaders of Gaul and tried to awaken their clergy to abuses, such as simony. Most dramatic, he sent missionaries to England. In Bede's mind this mission to England earned Gregory a 'greatness.' Whether or not it was a conscious policy, Gregory turned attention towards a new frontier in Europe that became the future of the Roman church in the West.

Gregory's papacy transformed the past and looked forward to a new age. Following a few notable previous bishops of Rome – Damasus, Innocent I,

Leo, and Gelasius – Gregory was an active pope, working on a variety of fronts. This is not to say that Gregory had a distinct vision or programme, perhaps of a Christian Europe set against Byzantium, or of an ecclesiastical government which might replace the secular powers. Gregory had no such plan; he acted as problems arose, following his own conscience and his sense of duty as *rector* responsible for the welfare of others and for the advancement of the Church. What shaped his actions most fundamentally was an eschatological perspective; an apocalyptic urgency. Knowing that God's severe judgement awaited, Gregory felt an anxious care to do what was right and to persevere.

A quotation from Paul the Deacon completes the portrait of this pope who accomplished much despite various adversities: 'He never rested, but was always engaged in providing for the interests of the people, or in writing down some composition worthy of the Church, or in searching out the secrets of heaven by the grace of contemplation' (*vita Greg.* 19). Gregory fulfilled his own restless command, '*Age quod agis!*'

APPENDICES

Gregory's works

Opera Omnia

The only edition of Gregory's entire works is in the *Patrologia Latina*, ed. J.-P. Migne (Paris 1878) vols 75–9. This edition reproduces unchanged that of the Maurists who used the sixteenth-century edition. Except for the *Homiliae in Evangelia*, these editions have been superseded, and will not be discussed.

The *Corpus Christianorum Series Latina* is in the process of editing Gregory's works. Occasionally, the *Sources chrétiennes* series will have the best Latin edition, as well as a French translation.

Registrum Epistularum

These letters cover the 14 years of Gregory's papacy. According to John the Deacon, to whom in the ninth century the original record was still available, Gregory's correspondence consisted of 14 individual papyrus books. Each codex covered one indiction, from 1 September to the end of the succeeding August. With a few exceptions that ultimately derive from the original letters copied at their point of arrival, all surviving letters of Gregory represent excerpts made from this Roman repository, the earliest being the group copied by Nothelm in Rome and inserted by Bede in his *Ecclesiastical History*. The main collections, known as P, C, and R, date from Carolingian times. Preservation has been adventitious (P has 54 letters, C has 2000 and R 684). The result is that we have 82 letters for book 1 (Indiction 9, September 590–August 591), the first year of Gregory's pontificate, and then for the successive years, 50 for Book 2, 65 for Book 3, 44 for Book 4, 63 for Book 5, 65 for Book 6, 41 for Book 7, 35 for Book 8, 240 for Book 9, 21 for Book 10, 59 for Book 11, 16 for Book 12, 49 for Book 13, and 17 for Book 14 (Indiction 7, September 603–March 604, the month of Gregory's death). Book 9 (Indiction 2, September 598–August 599) is the most fully preserved with 240 letters, and gives some sense of how busy Gregory's administration was. In the early seventh century the archive must have possessed thousands of letters.

Dag Norberg, the editor of Gregory's letters for the *Corpus Christianorum* series, divides the letters into three basic groups.[1] The first consists of personal letters which for reasons of their content must have been composed by Gregory himself. These would be letters such as 1.41 to Leander of Seville rejoicing over the conversion of

[1] Norberg 1980.

[41]

Reccared, or 3.64 to Theodore, the physician in Constantinople, lamenting the emperor's orders forbidding soldiers to enter religious orders. Gregory's own letters can be identified by their lack of rhythmic clausular endings. Unlike other Latin Fathers such as Jerome, Augustine and Cassiodore, who followed Cicero in ending their works with metric phrases, Gregory eschewed such ornamentation.

For purely administrative letters, Gregory depended on the help of his notaries, giving them either very summary or more detailed instructions, as the cases demanded. Within this group, two categories can be discerned. One category consists of letters written according to formulae whose phrases belong to an era preceding Gregory. Notaries probably learned these standard procedures on the job. (Later, books of exercises, *libri diurni*, would set out such standard forms). Letter 2.48 is such a formulaic letter written to reprimand Bishop Maximus of Syracuse for excommunicating Eusebius, a sick abbot. Other such formulae existed for ordering the election of new bishops (4.39), confirming them (3.11), or granting the pallium (6.18). A series of formulae covers the activities of the *defensores*, and other facets of administration of the patrimony. Another category of administrative letters treats special questions, is not repeated, and does not follow a set formulary. Instead, they have a distinctive preamble, exposition and disposition (*arenga, narratio* and *dispositio*). Letter 2.43, written about the Donatists, is such a letter. The form of these letters here reflects the notary's style, but from the content, it is clear that he is writing according to Gregory's instructions. Letters from the second and third group follow one of the three principal types of clausular endings (*cursus planus, tardus* or *velox*) most of the time.

Editions

S. Gregorii Magni Registrum Epistularum, ed. Dag Norberg. *CCL* 140–140A (Turnhout 1982). Norberg's studies (*In Registrum Gregorii Magni Studia Critica*) of 1937 and 1939, in which he examined both the manuscript tradition and the Latinity of the letters, underlie this edition. It includes only the letters that derive from the *Registrum* and contains no historical notes to eludicate the letters. See also Dag Norberg, *Criticial and Exegetical Notes of the Letters of St. Gregory the Great*, Filologiskarkiv 27 (Stockholm 1982).
Gregorii I papae Registrum epistularum I–II, ed. P. Ewald and L. Hartmann, 2 vols, *Monumenta Germaniae Historica. Epistulae* I–II (Berlin 1891–99). This edition has valuable notes and appendices. The numbering of the letters in Norberg's edition occasionally differs from that of the *MGH*, while the numbering of both these editions differs frequently from that of the Maurist edition (reprinted in *PL* 77). Of the letters not preserved in the *Registrum*, the *libellus responsionum* of Gregory to Augustine of Canterbury preserved by Bede should be considered authentic,[2] as should the third letter of Pelagius on the Three Chapters, written while Gregory was in Constantinople.[3]

---

[2] Meyvaert 1986.
[3] Meyvaert 1994.

Translations

Selected Epistles of Gregory the Great, repr. 1969, trans. Rev. James Barmby, *Nicene and Post-Nicene Fathers* 12–13 (Grand Rapids, Michigan 1969). Barmby has translated approximately 400 letters based on and with the numbering of the Maurist edition of Migne.

Grégoire le Grand, Registre des Lettres, intro., text, trans., notes and appends. Pierre Minard, 2 vols, Book I, *SC* 370; Book II, *SC* 371 (Paris 1991). Minard includes certain letters from the *MGH* edition as authentically Gregorian, and omits others, but otherwise follows the *CCL* text established by Dag Norberg.

Moralia in Iob Libri I–XXXV

Gregory's major work is an exegesis of the entire book of Job, begun after he was sent to Constantinople in 579 and preached to the monks who accompanied him there. In *Ep.* 1.41 (April 591) Gregory tells Leander he is sending volumes of his exposition of Job. The scribes are busying copying the work, but Gregory does not have a spare copy to send to his friend (*nisi portitoris ... festinatio coangustasset cuncta vobis transmittere ... voluissem*). He did not send Leander a copy until July 595 (*Ep.* 5.53), but even then this copy was not complete since Gregory did not have spare exemplars of Parts 3 (Books 11–16) and 4 (Books 17–22).

In the letter to Leander which prefaces the *Moralia*, Gregory explains more about the composition of the work. Leander and the brothers had asked Gregory to explicate not only the historical sense of the work, but also the allegorical sense, and to give the allegorical sense a moral import. Gregory delivered the first parts in their presence (*sub oculis*), and notes were taken by stenographers. Having more time free, he used dictation in treating the latter parts. When he revised, he added many things, and subtracted a few things. He corrected the earlier oral discourses to make them seem more like the dictated ones and vice versa. He mentions that the third part remains unrevised (Books 11–22; cf. *Mor.* 10.31.55; *Mor.* 11.1.1). The book was divided into six books of 35 chapters (Books 1–5, 6–10, 11–16, 17–22, 23–27, 28–35). That Gregory continued to make revisions is witnessed by his mention of the conversion of the English in *Mor.* 22.11.21 (Augustine's mission to Britain did not begin until 596).

While literal, Christological, and anagogical levels of exegesis are present, Gregory is most interested in the moral and ecclesiological meanings of the text: how Job represents the good Christian, the elect, or the Church itself. As such, the *Moralia* is a compendium of his spiritual teachings, and was for medieval monks and preachers a manual of moral, ascetic and mystical advice and inspiration. The *Moralia*'s popularity stemmed from its sensitive treatment of universal themes: if God is good, why is there evil? What is the meaning of suffering and how should one deal with it? How should one face the frightening, indeed, the apocalyptic disorder of one's times?

Gregory's answers build on tradition. He has an Augustinian appreciation of God's omnipotence and man's sinfulness, and freely confesses that God was the source of both the blessing and the afflictions man suffers. But the monastic tradition of the Desert Fathers and Cassian shape Gregory's reading of Augustine, so that body is more sharply set against the soul: suffering of the body could be used, even cultivated, for spiritual benefit. His belief in the power of reason and ascetic self-discipline is also a legacy of desert monasticism. Gregory's particular insight is the absolute mystery of God's visitations: is comfort and prosperity sent to reward the soul, or tempt it to damnation? Is adversity chastisement to heal the soul, or merely the beginning of punishment? To deal with this uncertainty, Gregory outlines how Christians can maintain a healthy equilibrium of soul in humility and hope. Stoic ideas of balance and moderation afford practical solutions for the challenges of daily life: the need to reconcile activity and contemplation, service to neighbour and individual purity, the bearing of power and the command of humility. Penitence and 'compunction' become a permanent inward disposition because of the uncertainty of God's judgement and the impossibility of knowing either one's own sinfulness or the sufficiency of one's penance. Hope can be maintained (for a salutary fear never permits security) by offering all one's actions as sacrifices to God. Much of Gregory's contribution lies in offering answers and practical strategies to help Christians deal with the uncertainties and spiritual dilemmas they faced.

Editions

S. Gregorii Magni Moralia in Iob, ed. Marcus Adriaen. *CCL* 143, 143A, 143B (Turnhout 1979–85). Approximately 500 manuscripts of the *Moralia* are extant. Adriaen consulted the Maurist text and 26 manuscripts used for that edition, plus eight additional manuscripts, valuable because of their antiquity or location. Finally, Adriaen compared codices of indirect tradition, and the oldest compilations of the *Moralia*: Paterius's *Liber testimoniorum*, which was composed in Gregory's time; the *elogia* of Lathcentius (d. 661); *libri sententiarum V* of Taio of Saragossa (bishop 651–83).

Translations

S. Gregory the Great, Morals on the Book of Job, trans., anon., 4 vols, *The Library of the Fathers* (Oxford 1844).
Grégoire le Grand, Morales sur Job, intro. and notes, Robert Gillet; trans. André de Gaudemaris, 3rd ed. 1 vol., Books I–II, *SC* 32 bis (Paris 1989). This edition uses the *CCL* text.
Grégoire le Grand, Morales sur Job, intro. and text, trans. and notes, Aristide Bocognano, 2 vols, Books XI–XIV, *SC* 212; Books XV–XVI, *SC* 221 (Paris 1974–75)
These editions use the text from the *PL*, with corrections.

Regula pastoralis liber

Written between September 590 and February 591, this work was used by Gregory in his synodical letter to the eastern patriarchs (*Ep.* 1.24). The *Regula pastoralis liber* is a response to John, the Bishop of Ravenna, who had criticized Gregory's reluctance to assume the office of pope. Gregory's Greek sources of inspiration include Origen's *Homilies on Ezechiel* and Gregory of Nazianzen's *Discourse 2,* on his flight from office, both known through translations by Rufinus. Parallels exist with John Chrysostom's book, *On the Priesthood*. Of Latin sources, one finds Seneca's moral essays and letters to Lucilius, Ambrose's *De officiis ministrorum*, and of Augustine, especially the *De catechizandis rudibus*. Gregory may have known Julianus Pomerius's *De Vita contemplativa*, but this cannot be proved absolutely.

This systematic work has the quality of a handbook. Through an extended analysis of the practice of the Stoic virtues of discretion, moderation and self-control, Gregory outlines the psychological strategies needed to achieve effective governance of oneself and of others. The *Regula pastoralis* has two versions, the earliest with a consecutive numbering of 68 chapters. Gregory then divided the work into four parts, as is noted in his prefatory letter to John of Ravenna. The first part discusses the kind of man fit to rule: a humble, contemplative man who has conquered the flesh and has no fears of worldly adversity. Part two discusses the *rector*'s way of life, which bends to his neighbours in sympathy but rises above them in contemplation. The ruler must especially be able to discriminate vices from virtues. The third and largest part addresses the problem of how the ruler should moderate his advice to various members of his audience. These subjects are listed as complementary opposites: rich and poor, proud and humble, male and female, old and young, etc. Specific advice is given on how authoritative severity should be balanced with merciful encouragement to meet the needs of the individual. A brief conclusion is given in the fourth part, admonishing the ruler to return to contemplation and introspection after the exercise of power. Such a recognition of one's own weakness restores a penitential disposition and ensures humility. This book of practical advice exercised great influence over the next ten centuries, and is virtually unique in its genre. Its circulation was wide. Anastasius II, the Patriarch of Antioch (599–609), translated it into Greek, but this translation is no longer extant. King Alfred of England had his own edition. Later missionaries, such as Ricci in China and Nobili in India, made use of it in the conversion of non-believers to Christianity.

Editions

A critical edition by F. Rommel and R.W. Clement is in preparation in the *CCL* series, see below.

Translations

Gregory the Great, *Pastoral Care*, trans. and annot. Henry Davis, *Ancient Christian Writers* 12 (Westminster, Maryland 1959).
Grégoire le Grand, Règle Pastorale, intro. notes and index, Bruno Judic; critical text, Floribert Rommel; trans. Charles Morel, 2 vols, *SC* 381, 382 (Paris 1992). This edition prints the text edited by F. Rommel and R.W. Clement to appear in the *CCL* series. The text here is based on a singularly important manuscript (Troyes, Ms 504, Bibliothèque Municipale de Troyes). This is a contemporary witness of the late sixth or early seventh century, probably of Italian origin; it may have been produced for the pope himself. Two further important and early manuscripts have been collated: Ivrea, Biblioteca Capitolare 1 (1) from the provenance of Luxeuil in the seventh to eighth century; and Paris, B.N. Lat. 9561 of the eighth century from England or Saint-Bertin.

Homiliae in Hiezechihelem prophetam

These homilies were preached before a monastic audience. The first 12 on the beginning of Ezechiel may date from as early as 591–92. The final ten on Chapter 40 have a *terminus ad quem, circa* 593, depending on the seige of Agilulf, the exact date of which is unknown. Gregory laments the destruction in Italy in 1.9.9; mentions Agilulf in *HEz.* 2.Prae., and alludes to the seige in his sudden ending in *HEz.* 2.10.24. Gregory collected the homilies in 601; the dedicatory letter is addressed to Marinianus, Bishop of Ravenna. During the period of time before the publication of the homilies, Gregory's secretary Paterius had composed his *liber testimoniorum*, a commentary on Biblical books in their correct order, drawing on the works of Gregory. Paterius quotes some passages from the homilies which Gregory later dropped when revising the manuscript. Thus Paterius has preserved some Gregorian texts otherwise unknown.

This book addresses exegesis and prophecy more deliberately than other works, and is richest in numerical symbolism and inventiveness of interpretation. Gregory seeks to unlock the mysterious symbolism to see how it reveals various teachings about Christ, history, the Church, spiritual life, etc. Ezechiel means *fortitudo Dei*, the strength of God; and the prophet Ezechiel is the type of the holy preacher who must face various problems in caring for his subjects and preserving the integrity of his own soul. He must himself balance active and contemplative lives, discriminate virtue from vice, 'digest' the scripture and preach its sweetness. He must be the 'watchman of Israel' discerning vices and rebuking the guilty. He must always preserve inner compunction; his whole life is a sacrifice to God (*HEz.* 2.8.14ff; 2.9.1ff). Jerusalem is the Church with its three orders: pastors, continent, and married, each possessing virtues shared in concord. Christological exegesis is important. Christ is especially the Mediator of God and man; his two natures are symbolized by *electrum*. He combined active and contemplative lives perfectly. While Christians must imitate Christ's perfection, they must thank God for his grace, for it is through grace that even sinners, through penitence, can come to perfection (*HEz.* 2.6.24).

Edition

S. Gregorii Magni Homiliae in Hiezechihelem prophetam, ed. Marcus Adriaen, 1 vol., *CCL* 142 (Turnhout 1971). Adriaen recognizes as most useful the text established by the Maurist Denys de Sainte-Marthe (*PL* 76, 785–1072) which used especially French manuscripts. Adriaen collated eight other early manuscripts with the Maurist edition. Twenty-three other manuscript variants are noted in the apparatus, along with collations from Paterius, Taio, Bede, Hrabanus Maurus and John the Deacon.

Translation

Grégoire le Grand, Homélies sur Ézéchiel, intro., Latin text, trans, and notes, Charles Morel, 2 vols, Book I, *SC* 327; Book II, *SC* 360 (Paris 1986–90). Morel reprints the *CCL* text with minor changes. He also notes variant readings in his apparatus.

Homiliae in Evangelia

Along with the *Dialogues*, these 40 homilies are Gregory's most accessible works. The language is unadorned, exegetical digressions are few, and the message is direct and easily comprehensible. Some passages and stories are later echoed in *Dialogues*. The sermons were preached to the clergy and people of Rome in 593; however, the assignment of churches given in Migne should not be trusted. The homilies are divided into two books, 20 in each, and a story underlies that division. The first 20 represent homilies Gregory dictated beforehand to a secretary who then read the homily at the appropriate moment of the mass. Gregory's excuse for doing this was his poor health. But the Roman people were unhappy with this procedure and complained. They wanted to hear Gregory himself speak. So the last 20 represent sermons given extemporaneously and taken down by notaries as Gregory spoke. Gregory may have chosen the first method of delivery less for reasons of health than of art. The former method gave Gregory more control over the text. Remarks in his dedicatory letter to Bishop Secundinus might be combined with the opening of Homily 21: '*multis vobis lectionibus per dictatum loqui consuevi, sed quia lassescente stomacho, ea quae dictavero legere ipse non possum, quosdam vestrum minus libenter audientes intueor. Unde nunc a memetipso exigere contra morem volo ut inter sacra missarum lectionem sancti Evangelii non dictando, sed solloquendo edisseram*'.

Because these homilies are on the Gospel, they are extremely useful in delineating finer points of Christology; yet they are fundamentally sermons directed at the moral reform of the audience. Typical Gregorian themes emerge. Christians must preserve their virtues with humility, the root of all good works; the dangers of pride loom large. Charitable works, chastity and rejection of the world are emphasized, as is constancy in adversity and prosperity. Christians must offer sacrifices of their thought on the altar of their hearts; and sacrifices of deeds of self-mortification. The theme of penitence and compunction stands out especially. Seeking to reform his audience, Gregory places much emphasis on the fear of judgement and the future punishment of sins. His repeated message is for sinners to repent with heartfelt tears and to amend their ways before the Lord comes at that unknown hour.

Editions

Sancti Gregorii Magni XL Homiliarum in Evangelia, ed. J. -P. Migne, *PL* 76, 1075–1312 (Paris 1878). The oldest manuscript is Roman, Cod. Lateran 1674 and is correlated with later manuscripts from Germany in the ninth century, and several later medieval manuscripts principally from France. The editors also consulted old editions from Antwerp, 1509, and two from Paris, dating from 1518 and 1571.

An edition is in preparation for the *CCL* by Raymond Étaix.

Translation

Gregory the Great, *Forty Gospel Homilies*, trans. Dom David Hurst, Cistercian Studies 123 (Kalamazoo, Michigan 1990). Numbering differs from that given in Migne.

Dialogi de vita et miraculis patrum Italicorum

Written before November of 594, the four books of the *Dialogues* present Gregory's teaching in a didactic question and answer format. Some of the anecdotes are second-hand, having their models in the Lives of the Desert Fathers: Cassian, Sulpicius Severus, Gregory of Tours, and others. Peter the Subdeacon is Gregory's interlocutor, and he complains that the world seems bereft of living saints. Gregory's answer sets out a cogent portrait of holiness, presenting the quotidian virtues of Christian life: charity, obedience, and discipline of the flesh. An important theme is authority: Gregory integrates the *rector*, the ruler bearing power, with the holy man. Saints are placed firmly within the Church, very often as bishops, priests and abbots. Holiness lies in oneness with God; saints cling and remain fixed in him, participating in his goodness. Saints achieve moral stability by obediently submitting their will to God and letting God govern their soul. Books One and Three consider saints in Italy and its environs, while Book Two is devoted to the life of St Benedict. Book Four deals with theological issues: how can the soul live on after the body dies? Is there corporal fire in hell? Is there a cleansing fire after death? Is there any way to help the soul of one departed? Gregory affirms the existence of a purifying fire to cleanse the soul of minor sins, and he extols the virtues of masses for the dead. The book was translated into Greek by Pope Zacharias (741–52), and later into Arabic and Anglo-Saxon.

The *Dialogues* are the subject of the most serious controversy in Gregorian studies. The authenticity of the *Dialogues* was contested in the sixteenth century by certain Protestant theologians, such as Robert Cooke. The literary style of the work differs from that of Gregory's sermons and exegetical works, and the work contains stories some have considered simplistic and superstitious. Particularly at issue were elements of a work-religion (*ergismus*): masses for the dead, purging fire, uses of the Eucharist, etc. In a two-volume study, *The Pseudo-Gregorian Dialogues*,[4] Francis Clark argues that the *Dialogues* were forged. Clark admits that they do contain some 80 Gregorian passages, whose authenticity is verified either by parallel passages in other of Gregory's writings, or by close similarity of wording and theme. Clark believes that these passages were edited out of Gregory's works as he corrected them, and preserved in chests in the *scrinium* (the papal archives). Sometime between 670 and 686, a cleric of the *scrinium* decided to compose the work, eager to show the Greeks that the Italians had nothing to envy in the Greek saints. To make his book authoritative, the forger wove the discarded Gregorian passages into his own work. Clark's argument rests on the following: 1) Gregory's letter to Maximian mentioning the *Dialogues* (*Ep.* 3.50) is a forgery. 2) References to the *Dialogues* in the compilations of Paterius and Taio of Saragossa must be rejected. The references are either later interpolations, or drawn from the Gregorian excerpts preserved in the papal *scrinium*, or Paterius and Taio themselves are later writers. 3) Neither Isidore of Seville, nor Braulio of Saragossa, or the *Liber pontificalis* mention the *Dialogues* explicitly. 4) It is only toward the end of the seventh century that the *Dialogues* appear in lists of Gregory's works. 5) The language has barbarisms that are 'ungregorian'.

---

[4] Clark 1987.

Although some scholars who have not worked on Gregory have given Clark some credibility, those who have worked on Gregory are virtually unanimous in their rejection of his thesis (see Bibliography). The authenticity of Gregory's letter to Maximian has been upheld by word studies. Paterius was a real contemporary of Gregory, referred to in two of Gregory's letters (*Ep.* 5.26, 6.12); and there is no reason to dispute his attribution of quotations to the *Dialogues*. The existence of a storehouse of snippets of Gregory's unedited writings in the *scrinium* is based on a mistranslation of a remark by Paterius, nor is there any evidence that such a storehouse of snippets existed. Taio of Saragossa, who composed a book of testimonies (texts of the scripture with commentaries) based on Paterius's *Liber testimoniorum*, actually contains a preface to Ecclesiastes (5) taken directly from the *Dialogues*, proving that he had his own copy of the book. Isidore of Seville has a passage on spiritual martyrdom cognate with the *Dialogues*. Thus, Paterius, Taio, and Isidore are all witnesses to the existence of the *Dialogues* before the seventh century. 'Barbarisms', such as *inhianter* and *silenter* can be verified as Gregorian vocabulary through the use of the *Thesaurus Gregorii Magni*. Finally, the emphasis on the importance of the sacrifice of the Eucharist for the living and the dead, and other spiritual doctrines which Clark finds unacceptable, can be reconciled when the whole of Gregory's works are read carefully.

Edition

Gregorii Magni Dialogi Libri IV, ed. Umberto Moricca (Rome 1924). Moricca believed that only the oldest manuscripts could be used because of the early contamination of the text. He uses ten manuscripts of Italian provenance for his edition, while the Maurists had used 20 French manuscripts in the *PL* edition. In so doing, Moricca fails to take account of many good manuscripts. Moricca uses an eighth-century manuscript, Milan Ambrosianus B. 159 Sup. as his principal authority. This edition has peculiar orthography; Moricca proceeded on the principle that the oddest spellings were likely to be the most authentic.

Translations

Saint Gregory the Great, *Dialogues*, trans. Odo John Zimmerman, OSB, *Fathers of the Church* 39 (New York 1959).
Grégoire le Grand, Dialogues, intro., critical text and notes, Adalbert de Vogüé, trans. Paul Antin, 3 vols, *SC* 251, 260, 265 (Paris 1978–80). de Vogüé discusses the manuscript tradition in his authoritative Introduction. Awaiting the critical text of the *Corpus Christianorum*, de Vogüé has prepared an edition by collating the Moricca edition based on Italian manuscripts with the Maurist edition of *PL*, based on French manuscripts. Variant manuscript readings listed in either apparatus can often resolve difficulties. de Vogüé also utilized the Greek edition of Zacharias of the eighth century (z), readings from R. Mittermüller's 1880 edition of book II (z [z]), and fragments of the *Dialogues* edited by G. Waitz in 1878 (w), and consulted two texts used by the Maurists, Saint-Gall 213 (G), and Autun 20 (H).

Expositio in Canticum Canticorum

From a letter of January 602 (*Ep.* 12.6) sent by Gregory to John the Subdeacon, his representative at Ravenna, several things emerge: first, that some years earlier Gregory had discoursed on several books of Scripture (Proverbs, the Song of Songs, the Prophets, the first book of Kings, and the Heptateuch). At that time, Claudius, Abbot of Sts John and Stephen at Ravenna, then on a prolonged stay in Rome, had taken down Gregory's words as he spoke (594–98). When Claudius returned to Ravenna, he took his notes of Gregory's discourses with him, intending to prepare them for publication by recasting them into book form. Later, when Claudius was on another visit to Rome, he showed the Pope a specimen of his work. Gregory was displeased because he believed his thoughts had sometimes been inaccurately rendered. Gregory's letter of 602, written after the death of Claudius, was therefore aimed at recovering all the material on the early discourses still in Claudius's possession at the time of his death. Scholars once believed that Claudius had been a monk of Gregory's monastery in Rome and that the discourses mentioned in *Ep.* 12.6 belonged to the period before Gregory became bishop. But a close study of Gregory's correspondence placed Claudius's long sojourn with Gregory during his pontificate; Claudius was never a monk in Gregory's monastery.[5]

Only two works covered by Gregory's description survive, namely the fragment of a commentary on the Canticle of Canticles and a fully developed commentary on the first Book of Kings. Their authenticity was doubted until this century, but both are now considered authentic works of Gregory.[6] Rodrigue Bélanger, the editor of the *Sources chrétiennes* edition, has argued that Claudius has himself edited the text because it is more systematically organized than most of Gregory's works.

This is a brief work: only the exegesis of the first eight verses of the Canticle survive of a longer work. These discourses probably gained an early circulation among Gregory's admirers, since the letter which St Columbanus wrote to Gregory in 600 CE clearly implies that he had seen them: *'transmitte et Cantica canticorum ab illo loco, in quo dicit, "Ibo ad montem myrrhae et collem thuris" [Cant. 4:6] usque in finem'*. This shows that more was then in circulation than has now survived.

In this work, Gregory has been inspired by Augustine, Aponius, and especially by Origen (in Rufinus's translation). Gregory follows Origen in the structure of his commentary. Each verse is first applied to the Church and to Christ, and then to each individual soul. This mystical work exalts the contemplative life above the moral and natural lives (a division taken from Origen). Exterior signs and language lead the soul inward to the highest union in which the Lord becomes the spouse of the soul. The Church, which is also his spouse, is at the same time holy, yet sinful. The members of the Church must strive along their individual roads of perfection through the stages of the moral and natural lives until fear evolves to respect, and respect to unitive love.

---

[5] de Vogüé 1978; Meyvaert 1978–79.
[6] Capelle 1929; Verbraken 1965; Meyvaert 1978–79.

Edition

Sancti Gregorii Magni Expositio in Canticum Canticorum, ed. Patrick Verbraken, *CCL* 144 (Turnhout 1963). Verbraken discusses manuscripts in, 'La Tradition manuscripts du Commentaire de saint Grégoire sur le Cantique des Cantiques', *RB* 73 (1963), 277–88. In establishing the text, Verbraken used 21 manuscripts. Two main manuscript branches exist, the oldest dates from Gregory's time. Two manuscripts contain a commentary that Robert of Tombelaine composed in the second half of the eleventh century in an attempt to complete the work. This addition is what lead to doubts of the authenticity of Gregory's work which persisted until Capelle showed there was an authentic fragment linked by its title to the papal archives. The Maurist edition reprinted by Migne is based on manuscripts now lost, and the beginning of Gregory's commentary has been substituted with that of Robert of Tombelaine.

Translation

Grégoire le Grand, Commentaire sur le Cantique des Cantiques, intro., trans., notes and index Rodrigue Bélanger, 1 vol., *SC* 314 (Paris 1984). Bélanger reprints the *CCL* edition with emendations suggested by Meyvaert (1978–79).[7]

In librum primum Regum expositiones

Like the commentary on the Song of Songs (see preceeding entry), this work survives because of the notes of Claudius of Ravenna, who recast Gregory's discourses into a book form. While the substance of the work is Gregorian, there are also some non-Gregorian elements in the diction showing the intervention of Claudius. The preface, however, which is fully Gregorian in tone, suggests that Gregory himself may have made a final revision of the work before he died.

Gregory's work on Kings is his last exegetical production, and as the *Sources chrétiennes* editor Adalbert de Vogüé has argued, the book should be read in light of Gregory's political concerns with barbarian kings, as well as his usual spiritual considerations. Kings are royal and appointed by God, yet they should always seek advice from the spiritual *rector.* They, too, must be obedient to his advice.

Gregory's lengthy exposition is limited to the first 16 chapters of I Kings (=I Samuel). As in all exegetical works, digressions yield information on diverse points of doctrine. This work is closely devoted to problems of monastic life and contemplation, a sensibility that links it with the time period of his exegesis of the Song of Songs. Helcana represents the 'unified life' of one loving God alone; his two wives Anna and Phenenna represent the active and contemplative lives respectively, as do Mary and Martha, Rachel and Leah. Samuel, the son of Anna, is first a type of Christ, whose divine strength assumed weak humanity to redeem it. Samuel also represents the order of preachers, whose preaching and teaching of the sublime word to the weak brings them to God. While contemplation is exalted as the highest life, Gregory's work also deals with the responsibilities of service and the need for discretion to discern virtue and vice in daily activity. Gregory makes concessions to those who

[7] Meyvaert 1978–79.

cannot maintain themselves in the perfection of contemplation: one can contemplate the good works of others and be inspired by them. Samuel comes to represent the summit of perfection, pleasing God as well as men, serving God and neighbour. More than other works, this work emphasizes the absolute obedience characteristic of monastic life: Samuel obeys the orders and countermands of his superior willingly and without murmuring complaint.

Edition

Sancti Gregorii Magni In librum primum Regum expositiones, ed. Patrick Verbraken, 1 vol., *CCL* 144 (Turnhout 1963). Verbraken discusses the manuscript tradition in 'Le text du Commentaire sur les Rois attribué à saint Grégoire', *RB* 66 (1956), 39–62 and 'Le Commentaire de saint Grégoire sur le premier Livre des Rois', *RB* 66 (1956), 159–217. This edition is based on a single twelfth-century manuscript: CAVA *Badia* 9. Variants from the Maurist edition, and the Venice edition of 1537, whose original manuscript is now lost, are noted in the apparatus.

Translation

Grégoire le Grand, Commentaire sur le premier livre des Rois, intro., trans. and notes Adalbert de Vogüé, vol. 1, Preface II.28, *SC* 351 (Paris 1989).
Grégoire le Grand, Commentaire sur le premier livre des Rois, text, trans. and notes Christophe Vuillaume, vol. 2, Books II.29–III.37, *SC* 391 (Paris 1989–).
  These editions reprint the *CCL* text with minor corrections.

Denuntatio pro septiformi letania and Oratio sancti Gregorii ad plebem de mortalitate

These two texts are very similar. According to Gregory of Tours 10.1, Gregory preached the sermon or litany after his election, while the plague was still raging. Gregory sees the plague as the scourge of God (*flagellum Dei*) meant to discipline sinful people. Gregory calls for repentance and reform, summoning penitential processions from the major churches in Rome – John the Baptist, Marcellus, John and Paul, Cosmos and Damian, Stephen, Vitalis, and Caecilia – to converge on the Lateran basilica. A penitential procession might have been repeated during a later plague in 603.
  The *oratio* was included with manuscripts of the *Registrum Epistularum* and sometimes with the *Homiliae in Evangelia.* The original text is most likely that of Gregory of Tours, *Hist. Franc.* 10.1. Mention of the litany is made by Paul the Deacon, *de gestis Langob.* 50.3, and by John the Deacon, *vita Greg.* 1.42.

Editions

Denuntatio pro septiformi letania. S. Gregorii Magni, Registrum Epistularum, Append. IX, ed. Dag Norberg, *CCL* 140A, (Turnhout 1982), 1102–04. The *Denuntatio* comes down in a manuscript of the Registrum, Cod. R1 (Casin. 71), dating from the sixth indiction (603).
Denuntatio pro septiformi letania. Gregorii I papae Registrum epistularum, eds. P. Ewald and L. Hartmann, *MGH. Ep.* 2, 365–7 (Berlin 1891–1899).

Oratio sancti Gregorii ad plebem de mortalitate, ed. J. -P. Migne, *PL* 76, 1311–14, (Paris 1878).

Doubtful or spurious works

Sancti Gregorii Magni concordia quorumdam testimoniorum sacrae scripturae

This work takes certain texts of Paul and places them in opposition to seemingly contradictory passages from the Old or New Testaments. An *interrogatio* follows making explicit the disagreement of the texts. A *responsio* then reconciles the apparent contradictions. The aim is to prove: 'In these two testimonies, the two holy apostles are not at all dissonant, but are truly harmonious in dissonance' (*In his duobus testimoniis sancti duo apostoli omnino dissonant, sed dissonando ueraciter concordant.* 32.50.9–10). In the *concordia*, the sentence structure and the concerns are consonant with Gregory's works. The vocabulary is also Gregorian, as can be discovered by matching words and phrases using the CD-ROM from the CETEDOC Library of Christian Latin Texts. This work merits study, as it may be authentic.

Editions

Sancti Gregorii Magni concordia quorumdam testimoniorum sacrae scripturae, ed. J.-P. Migne, *PL* 79, 657–78. The Maurist edition reprinted by Migne is based on the sixteenth-century edition of the text by J. Gilot from a manuscript at Saint-Denys, now Paris B.N. lat. 2384, which they corrected with the aid of one manuscript, Tours Bibliothèque Muncipale ms. 20.

Irené Fransen, 'Trente-quatre questions sur saint-Paul passés sous le nom de saint Grégoire', *RB* 73 (1963), 244–76. In addition to the manuscripts used by the Maurists, other witnesses exist which are listed by Fransen. Fransen believes the *concordia* is of Irish origin, because of its heavy Augustinianism and its attitude toward penitence, discretion, and fraternal correction. Of course, others will argue these are very much Gregorian characteristics.

Another manuscript exists at the Houghton Library, Harvard University: fms TYP 495 (IXs.) Trier.

In Septem Psalmos Poenitentiales Expositio

This work probably dates from the twelfth century.

Edition

Ascribed to Gregory in *PL* 79, 549–658.

Sermo in Dominica Resurrectionis

Spurious, cf. E. Dekkers, *Clavis Patrum Latinorum* (Steenbrugge 1961) [=*Sacris erudiri* 3], 1721.

Edition

Ascribed to Gregory in *PL* 79, 549–678.

Sacramentarium Gregorianum

Charlemagne asked Pope Hadrian c.790 for a copy of the standard Roman Mass book and received one (known now as the 'Hadrianum'). The title ascribed the work to Gregory. Hadrian's covering letter also stated that Gregory was the author of this sacramentary. The actual MS sent to Charlemagne has not survived, but a copy made from it in 811 is preserved in Cambrai, Bibliothèque municipale MS 164. This manuscript is representative of a whole class of sacramentaries known to liturgical scholars as the Gregorian Sacramentary. Scholars are doubtful that Gregory himself was responsible for drawing up this particular liturgical book. But Dom Henry Ashworth has shown that close to a hundred prayers in this sacramentary, out of many times that number, were actually composed by Gregory. They bear the imprint of his vocabulary and literary style. The explanation probably lies in the fact that notaries took down Gregory's words, not only when he preached but also when he recited a prayer. Later these prayers were integrated into a sacramentary, probably thus lending the name of Gregory to this work.

While Gregory may not have written this sacramentary, he was interested in the liturgy and apparently made some changes. In *Ep.* 9.26 of October 598, Gregory wrote to John of Syracuse strongly defending himself against accusations of meddling with the liturgy to make it resemble more closely that of Constantinople.

Ascribed to Gregory in *PL* 78, 25–240.

Liber Responsalis sive Antiphonarius

In his life of Gregory (2.6), John the Deacon wrote that Gregory established a school of cantors, and admonished the boys with a whip to preserve the authentic Antiphonarius. The accuracy of this account has been debated, but whatever its veracity, John is evidence that the legend of Gregory was associated with the chant from at least the ninth century. Several strata of the music known as 'Gregorian Chant' can be discerned. There are at least four non-Gregorian parallels or antecedents: Ambrosian, Gallican, Mozarabic, and Old Roman. Some add a fifth, from Benevento. The ultimate origin is probably Antioch or Jerusalem. Some parts of the chant may have been stabilized around Gregory's era of the late sixth century.

Edition

Ascribed to Gregory in *PL* 78, 725–850.

SELECT BIBLIOGRAPHY

This is a select bibliography; works on Gregory are numerous. Readers now have available the indispensable work by Robert Godding, *Bibliografia di Gregorio Magno (1890–1989)*, Opere di Gregorio Magno, Complementi/1 (Rome 1990), which lists 2608 items.

Abbreviations to periodicals are from *L'Année Philologique*, supplemented with those from Johannes Quasten's *Patrology*.

Current bibliography

L'Année philologique.
Bulletin d'histoire bénédictine (supplement to the *Revue bénédictine).*
Bulletin Signalétique.
Bulletin de théologie ancienne et médiévale (supplement to the *Revue de théologie ancienne et médiévale).*
Medioevo Latino.
Revue d'histoire ecclésiastique.

Reference tools

CETEDOC Library of Christian Latin Texts Universitas Catholica Lovaniensis Lovanii Novi (Turnhout 1991), a CD-ROM.
Thesaurus Sancti Gregorii Magni, Series A, *Formae. Enumeratio formarum. Index formarum a tergo ordinatarum. Concordantia*, CETEDOC Universitas Catholica Lovaniensis Lovanii Novi, Corpus Christianorum, Thesaurus Patrum Latinorum (Turnhout 1986), 2 vols and 99 microfiches.

Reference works

Altaner, B. and Stuiber, A., *Patrologie. Leben. Schriften und Lehre der Kirchenväter,* (Freiburg im Breisgau, Basel, Vienna 1978), 466–472, 649–651.
Brunhölzl, F., *Geschichte der lateinischen Literatur des Mittelalters,* I, *Von Cassiodor bis zum Ausklang der karolingischen Erneuerung,* (Munich 1975) 25–66.
Dekkers, É. and Gaar, A., *Clavis Patrum Latinorum* (Steenbrugge 1961) n. 1708–23. [=*Sacris erudiri,* 3]
Frede, H. -J., *Kirchenschriftsteller. Verzeichnis und Sigel. Vetus Latina* I/1, (Freiburg im Breisgau 1981), 348–51.

Bibliographies

Godding, R., *Bibliografia di Gregorio Magno* (1890–1989), Opere di Gregorio Magno, Complementi/1 (Rome 1990).

Paronetto, V., 'Note gregoriane: A proposito di alcune recenti pubblicazioni su Gregorio Magno', *Rivista di Storia della Chiesa in Italia* 34 (1980), 174–87.

Recchia, V., 'Rassegna gregoriana', *Vetera Christianorum* 6 (1969), 177–99.

Recchia, V., 'Rassegna di studi su Gregorio Magno', *Vetera Christianorum* 10 (1973), 406–16.

Serenthà, L., 'Introduzione bibliografica allo studio di S. Gregorio Magno', *La scuola cattolica* 102 (1974), 283–301.

Colloquia

Grégoire le Grand, eds. Fontaine, J., Gillet, R., and Pellistrandi, S., Chantilly, Centre culturel les Fontaines, 15–19 septembre 1982, Colloques internationaux du Centre National de la Recherche Scientifique (Paris 1986).

Gregorio Magno e il suo tempo, ed. Grassi, V., XIX Incontro di studiosi dell'antichità cristiana in collaborazione con l'École Française de Rome, Roma, 9–12 maggio 1990, 2 vols (Rome 1991).

Gregory the Great: A symposium, ed. Cavadini, J.C., (Notre Dame 1996), forthcoming.

Settimane di Studio del Centro italiano di Studi sull'alto Medioevo (Spoleto 1953) See especially: vol. 9, *Il passaggio dall'Antichità al Medioevo in Occidente* (1962); vol. 14, *La conversióne al cristianesimo nell'Europa dell'Alto Medioevo* (1966); vol. 17, *La storiografia altomedievale* (1970); vol. 19, *La scuola nell'Occidente latino dell'Alto Medioevo* (1972); vol. 22, *La cultura antica nell'Occidente latino dal VII all XI secolo* (1975); vol. 23, *Simboli e simbologia nell'alto Medioevo* (1976).

Collections

Catry, P., *Parole de Dieu. Amour et Esprit-Saint chez saint Grégoire le Grand,* Vie Monastique 17 (Bellefontaine 1984).

Markus, R., *From Augustine to Gregory the Great* (London 1983).

Meyvaert, P., *Benedict, Gregory, Bede and Others* (London 1977).

de Vogüé, A., *Saint Benoît. Sa Vie et sa Règle. Études choisies,* Vie Monastique 12 (Bellefontaine 1981).

Encylopedia articles

Gillet, R., 'Grégoire le Grand', *Dictionnaire de Spiritualité,* vol. 6 (Paris 1967), 872–910.

Gillet, R., 'Grégoire le Grand', *Dictionnaire d'histoire et de géographie ecclésiastiques,* vol. 21 (Paris 1986), 1387–1420.

Manselli, R., 'Gregor der Grosse', *Reallexikon für Antike und Christentum,* vol. 12 (Stuttgart 1983), 93–951.

Markus, R., 'Gregor I, der Grosse', *Theologische Realenzyklopädie,* vol. 14 (Berlin and New York 1985), 135–45.

Meyvaert, P., 'Gregory I', *The Encylopedia of Religion,* vol. 6 (New York and London 1987), 118–21.

Recchia, V., 'Gregorio Magno', *Dizionario degli scrittori greci e latini,* vol. 2 (Settimo Milanese 1988), 1121–32.

Rush, A., 'Gregory I (The Great)', *New Catholic Encyclopedia,* vol. 6 (Washington 1967–79), 766–70.

General historical context

Bertolini, O., *Roma di fronte a Bisanzio e ai Longobardi* (Bologna 1941), 231–284.

Brown, T.S., *Gentlemen and Officers: Imperial Administration and Aristocratic Power in Byzantine Italy, A.D. 554–800)* (Rome 1984).

Diehl, C., *Études sur l'administration Byzantine de l'exarchat de Ravenne* (Paris 1888).

Guillou, A., *Régionalisme et indépendance dans l'empire Byzantine au VIIe siècle: L'example de l'exarchat et de la Pentapole d'Italie* (Rome 1969).

Guillou, A., 'L'Éveque dans la société méditerranéenne des VIe–VIIe siècles. Un modèle', *Bibliothèque de l'École des Chartres* 131 (1973), 5–19.

Guillou, A., *Culture et Société en Italie Byzantine* (London 1978).

Jones, A.H.M., *The Later Roman Empire,* 2 vols. (Norman, Oklahoma 1964).

Le Goff, J., *La civilisation de l'occident médiéval* (Paris 1964).

Llewellyn, P., *Rome in the Dark Ages* (London 1970).

Riché, P., *L'Europe barbare de 476 à 774* (Paris 1989).

Ward-Perkins, B., *From Classical Antiquity to the Middle Ages: Urban Public Building in Northern and Central Italy A.D. 300–850* (Oxford 1984).

Biographies

Battifol, P., *Saint Gregory the Great,* trans. J. Stoddard (New York 1929).

Battistelli, V., *Consul Dei: San Gregorio Magno. La Via 5* (Alba-Roma 1942).

Dudden, F.H., *Gregory the Great: His Place in History and Thought,* 2 vols. (London, New York and Bombay 1905).

Gandolfo, E., *Gregorio Magno, servo dei servi di Dio* (Milan 1980).

Manselli, R., *Gregorio Magno* (Turin 1967).

Markus, R.A., *Gregory the Great and His World* (Cambridge 1997), forthcoming.

Minard, P., Lefevre, G., and Doucet, M., 'Saint Grégoire le Grand', *Lettre de Ligugé* 221 (1983), 6–42.

Paronetto, V., *Gregorio Magno. Un maestro alle origini cristiane d'Europa* (Rome 1985).

Richards, J., *Consul of God: The Life and Times of Gregory the Great* (London 1980).

Synthetic intellectual histories

Dagens, C., *Saint Grégoire le Grand. Culture et expérience chrétiennes* (Paris 1977).
Straw, C., *Gregory the Great,* Perfection in Imperfection (Berkeley 1988)
Weber, L., *Hauptfragen der Moraltheologie Gregors des Grossen* (Freiburg in der Schweiz 1947).

Economy and society

Bavant, B., *'Le duché byzantin de Rome. Origine, durée et extension géographique'* *Mélanges de l'École française de Rome* Moyen Age – Temps modernes 91 (1979), 41–88.
Boesch Gajano, S., 'Dislivelli culturali e mediazioni ecclesiastiche nei "Dialogi" di Gregorio Magno', *Quaderni storici* 41 (1979), 398–415.
Guillou, A., 'Trasformazione delle strutture socio-economiche nel mondo bizantino dal VI all'VIII sècolo', *Quaderni medievali* 8 (1979), 106–15.
Hannestad, K., *L'evolution des ressources agricoles de l'Italie du IVe au VIe siècle de notre ère* (Copenhagen 1962).
Heitz, C., 'Les monuments de Rome à l'époque de Grégoire le Grand', *Grégoire le Grand* (Paris 1986), 31–40, [see Colloquia].
McNally, R.E., 'Gregory the Great (590–604) and His Declining World', *Archivum Historiae Pontificiae* 16 (1978), 7–26.
Pepe, G., *Il Medioevo barbarico d'Italia* (Turin 1942).
Pietri, C., 'L'Église de Rome, les clercs et l'aristocratie au temps de Grégoire le Grand', *Grégoire le Grand* (Paris 1986), 107–22 [see Colloquia].
Pietri, C., 'La Rome de Grégoire', *Gregorio Magno e il suo tempo* (Rome 1991), vol. 1, 9–32 [see Colloquia].
Recchia, V., *Gregorio Magno e la Società agricola,* Verba Seniorum, NS 8 (Rome 1978).
Rouche, M., 'Grégoire le Grand et l'économie de son temps', *Grégoire le Grand* (Paris 1986), 41–58 [see Colloquia].
Ruggini, L., *Economia e Società nella 'Italia annonaria'* (Milan 1961).
Wickham, C., *Early Medieval Italy* (Totowah, New Jersey 1981).

Gregory and the East

Cracco Ruggini, L., 'Grégoire le Grand et le monde byzantine', *Grégoire le Grand* (Paris 1986), 83–94 [see Colloquia].
Dagens, C., 'L'Église universelle et le monde oriental chez saint Grégoire le Grand', *Istina* 20 (1975), 457–75.
Fischer, E.H., 'Gregor der Grosse und Byzanz: Ein Beitrag zur Geschichte der päpstlichen Politik', *Zeitschrift der Savigny Stiftung für Rechtsgeschichte. Kanonistische Abteilung* 36 (1950), 15–144.
Maraval, P., 'Grégoire le Grand et les Lieux Saints de l'Orient', *Gregorio Magno e il suo tempo* (Rome 1991), vol. 1, 65–76 [see Colloquia].
Recchia, V., 'I protagonisti dell'offensiva romana antimonofisita tra la fine del quinto

e i primi decenni del sesto secolo dai *Dialoghi* di Gregorio Magno', *Grégoire le Grand* (Paris 1986), 159–70 [see Colloquia].

Tuilier, A., 'Grégoire le Grand et le titre de patriarche oecuménique', *Grégoire le Grand* (Paris 1986), 69–82 [see Colloquia].

Gregory as pope

Batany, J., 'Le vocabulaire des fonctions sociales et ecclésiastiques chez Grégoire le Grand', *Grégoire le Grand* (Paris 1986), 171–80 [see Colloquia].

Boesch Gajano, S., 'Per una storia degli Ebrei in Occidente tra Antichità e medioevo. La testimonianza di Gregorio Magno', *Quaderni medievali* 8 (1979), 12–43.

Caspar, E., *Geschichte des Papsttums von den Anfängen bis zur Höhe der Weltherrschaft,* vol. 2 (Tübingen 1933), 306–514.

Chadwick, H., 'Gregory the Great and the Mission to the Anglo-Saxons', *Gregorio Magno e il suo tempo,* vol. 1 (Rome 1991), 199–212 [see Colloquia].

Consolino, F.E., 'I Doveri del principe cristiano nel *Registrum Epistularum* di Gregorio Magno', *Ricerche patristiche in onore di Dom Basil Studer. Augustinianum* 33 (1993), 57–82.

Duval, Y., 'Grégoire et l'Église d'Afrique: les "hommes" du Pape', *Gregorio Magno e il suo tempo,* vol. 1 (Rome 1991), 129–58 [see Colloquia].

Eno, R., *The Rise of the Papacy,* (Wilmington, Delaware 1990).

Gasparri, S., 'Gregorio Magno e l'Italia Meridionale', *Gregorio Magno e il suo tempo,* vol 1 (Rome 1991), 77–101 [see Colloquia].

Gaudemet, J., 'Aspects de la primauté romaine du Vè au XVè siècle, *Ius canonicum* 22 (1971), 92–134.

Guillou, A., 'L'Évêque dans la société méditerranéenne des VIe–VIIe siècles. Un Modèle', *Bibliothèque de l'École des Chartres* 131 (1973), 5–20.

Jones, A.H.M., 'Church Finance in the Fifth and Sixth Centuries', *Journal of Theological Studies* 11 (1960), 84–94.

Katz, S., 'Pope Gregory the Great and the Jews', *The Jewish Quarterly Review* 24 (1933), 113–36.

Kopka, G., 'The Pope as a Diplomat: A Study of Selected Correspondence of Gregory the Great with Secular Authorities of his Day', Diss. University of Texas, (Austin, Texas 1967).

Lanzoni, F., *Le diocesi d'Italia dalle origini al secolo VII (604),* Studi e testi 35 (Faenza 1927).

Llewellyn, P., 'The Roman Church in the Seventh Century: The Legacy of Gregory the Great', *Journal of Ecclesiastical History* 25 (1974), 363–80.

Markus, R.A., 'Donatism: The Last Phase', *Studies in Church History* 1, eds. C.W. Dugmore and C. Duggan (Leiden 1964), 118–26 = *From Augustine to Gregory the Great,* (London 1983), ch.VI, [see Collections].

Markus, R., 'Reflections on Religious Dissent in North Africa in the Byzantine Period', *Studies in Church History,* 3 (1966), 140–49; ed. G.J. Cuming = *From Augustine to Gregory the Great,* (London 1983), ch. VII, [see Collections].

Markus, R., 'Gregory the Great and Papal Missionary Strategy', *The Mission of the Church and the Propagation of the Faith,* Studies in Church History 6 (1970),

29–38; ed. G.J. Cuming = *From Augustine to Gregory the Great* (London 1983), ch. IX [see Collections].

Markus, R., 'Christianity and Dissent in Roman North Africa in the Byzantine Period', *Studies in Church History* 9 (1972), 21–36; ed. D. Baker = *From Augustine to Gregory the Great* (London 1983), ch. VIII [see Collections].

Markus, R., 'The Cult of Images in Sixth Century Gaul', *Journal of Theological Studies*, ns. 29 (1978), 151–57 =*From Augustine to Gregory the Great* (London 1983), ch. XII [see Collections].

Markus, R., 'The Problem of "Donatism" in the sixth century', *Gregorio Magno e il suo Tempo*, vol. 1 (Rome 1991), 159–66 [see Colloquia].

Meyvaert, P., 'Gregory the Great and the Theme of Authority', *Benedict, Bede and Others* (London 1977), Ch. V, 3–12 [see Collections].

Pietri, L., 'Grégoire le Grand et la Gaule: le projet pour la réforme de l'Église Gauloise', *Gregorio Magno e il suo tempo*, vol. 1 (Rome 1991), 109–128 [see Colloquia].

Reydellet, M., *La royauté dans la littérature latine, de Sidoine Apollinaire à Isidore de Séville* (Rome 1981).

Sharkey, N., *St Gregory the Great's Concept of Papal Primacy*, Diss. Catholic University of America (Washington 1950).

Straw, C., 'Gregory's Politics; Theory and Practice', *Gregorio Magno e il suo tempo*, vol. 1 (Rome 1991), 47–63 [see Colloquia].

Ullmann, W., *The Growth of Papal Government. A Study in the Ideological Relation of Clergy to Lay Power*, second ed. (London 1962).

Ullmann, W., *A Short History of the Papacy in the Middle Ages* (London 1972).

Vilella Masana, J., 'Gregorio Magno e Hispania', *Gregorio Magno e il suo tempo*, vol. 1 (Rome 1991), 167–86 [see Colloquia].

Walther, M., *Pondus, Dispensatio, Dispositio* (Kriens 1941).

Gregory as writer

Bartelink, G., 'Pope Gregory the Great's Knowledge of Greek', trans. P. Meyvaert, *Gregory the Great: A Symposium* (Notre Dame 1996), forthcoming [see Colloquia].

Capelle, D.P., 'Les Homilies de saint Grégoire le grand sur le Cantique', *Revue Bénédictine* 41 (1929), 204–17.

Courcelle, P., '*Habitare secum* selon Perse et selon S. Grégoire le Grand', *Revue des études anciennes* 69 (1967), 266–79.

Courcelle, P., 'S. Grégoire à l'école de Juvénal', *Studi in onore di Alberto Pincherle* (Rome 1967b), 170–74.

Courcelle, P., *Late Latin Writers and Their Greek Sources,* trans. H.E. Wedeck (Cambridge, Mass. 1969).

Dagens, C., 'Grégoire le Grand et la culture: de la *sapientia hujus mundi* à la *docta ignorantia* ', *Revue des études augustiniènnes* 14 (1968), 17–26.

Dekkers, É., '"Discretio" chez Benoît et saint Grégoire', *Collectanea Cisterciensia* 46 (1984), 79–88.

Fontaine, J., *Isidore de Séville et la culture classique dans l'Espagne wisigothique*, second ed. 3 vols. (Paris 1983).

Gastaldelli, F., 'Osservazioni per un profilo letterario di San Gregorio Magno', *Salesianum* 26 (1964), 441–61.

Hesbert, R.J., 'Le bestiaire de Grégoire', *Grégoire le Grand* (Paris 1986), 455–66 [see Colloquia].

Lubac, H. de, *Exégèse médiévale. Les quatre sens de l'Écriture,* Coll. Théologie 41–42 (Paris 1959–61).

McClure, J., 'Gregory the Great: Exegesis and Audience', D.Phil. diss. Oxford University (Oxford 1978).

Meyvaert, P., 'The Date of Gregory the Great's Commentaries on the Canticle of Canticles and on I Kings', *Sacris erudiri* 23 (1978–79), 191–216.

Meyvaert, P., 'Le libellus responsionum à Augustin de Cantorbéry: une oeuvre authentique de saint Grégoire le Grand' (Paris 1986), 543–50 [see Colloquia].

Meyvaert, P., 'A Letter of Pelagius II Composed by Gregory the Great', *Gregory the Great: A Symposium* (Notre Dame 1996), forthcoming, ed. J.C. Cavadini [see Colloquia].

Norberg, D., 'Qui a composé les lettres de saint Grégoire le Grand?', *Studi medievali* 21 (1980), 1–17.

Norberg, D., *Critical and Exegetical Notes on the Letters of St Gregory the Great,* Kungl Vitterhets, Historie och Antikvitets Akademien, Filologisk arkiv 27 (Stockholm 1982).

Norberg, D., 'Style personnel et style administratif dans le *Registrum epistularum* de saint Grégoire le Grand', *Grégoire le Grand* (Paris 1986), 489–98 [see Colloquia].

O'Malley, B., *The Animals of St Gregory,* Intr. J. Leclercq (Rhandirmwyn 1981).

Paronetto, V., 'Gregorio Magno e la cultura classica', *Studium* 74 (1978), 665–80.

Petersen, J., 'Did Gregory the Great Know Greek?',*The Orthodox Churches and the West,* ed. D. Baker (Oxford 1976), 121–134.

Peterson, J., 'Homo omnino Latinus? The Theological and Cultural Background of Pope Gregory the Great', *Speculum* 62 (1987), 529–51.

Riché, P., *Education and Culture in the Barbarian West. Sixth through Eighth Centuries,* trans. J.J. Contreni (Columbia, South Carolina 1976).

Sepulcri, A., 'Gregorio Magno e la scienza profana', *Atti della Reale Accademia delle scienze di Torino* 39 (1903–04), 962–76.

Verbraken, P., 'La tradition manuscrit du Commentaire de S.Grégoire sur le Cantique des Cantiques', *Revue bénédictine* 73 (1963), 277–88.

Verbraken, P., 'Un nouveau manuscrit du Commentaire de S.Grégoire sur le Cantique des Cantiques (Ms. Düsseldorf, Landes-u. Stadtbibliothek B3, f° 133–159v°), *Revue bénédictine* 75 (1965), 143–45.

Vinay, G., *Alto medioevo latino: Conversazioni e no* (Napoli 1978), 11–82.

de Vogüé, A., 'Grégoire le Grand Lecteur de Grégoire de Tours?', *Analecta Bollandiana* 94 (1976), 225–33.

Spirituality

Aubin, P., 'Intériorité et extériorité dans les *Moralia in Job* de saint Grégoire le Grand', *Revue des science religieuse* 62 (1974), 117–66.

Baus, K., Beck, H.G., Ewig, E. and Vogt, H.J., *History of the Church*, vol. 2, *The Imperial Church from Constantine to the Early Middle Ages,* trans, Biggs, A. (New York 1969), 602–756.

Bélanger, R., 'Introduction', *Grégoire le Grand. Commentaire sur le Cantique des Cantiques, SC* 314 (Paris 1984), 11–62.

Boglioni, P., 'Miracle et nature chez Grégoire le Grand', *Cahiers d'études médiévales.* I, *Epopées, légends et miracles* (Montréal and Paris 1974).

Bouyer, L., Leclercq, J. and Vandenbroucke, F., *A History of Christian Spirituality,* vol. 2, Leclercq, J., *The Spirituality of the Middle Ages,* trans. The Benedictines of Holme Eden Abby, Carlisle (New York 1961), 3–30.

Dagens, C., 'La fin des temps et l'Église selon saint Grégoire le Grand', *Revue des science religieuse* 58 (1970), 273–88.

Frickel, M., *Deus Totus Ubique Simul: Untersuchungen zur allgemeinen Gottgegenwart im Rahmen der Gotteslehre Gregors des Grossen* (Freiburg im Breisgau 1956).

Gastaldelli, F., 'Il Meccanismo Psicologico del Peccato nei *Moralia in Job* di San Gregorio Magno', *Salesianum* 27 (1965), 563–605.

Gastaldelli, F., 'Prospettive sul Peccato in San Gregorio Magno', *Salesianum* 28 (1966), 64–94.

Gillet, R., 'Introduction', *Grégoire le Grand. Morales sur Job, Sources chrétiennes* 32 (1952), 7–113.

Gramaglia, P.A., 'Linguaggio sacrificale ed eucarestia in Gregorio Magno', *Gregorio Magno e il suo tempo,* vol. 2 (Rome 1991), 223–65, [see Colloquia].

Leclercq, J., *The Love of Learning and the Desire for God: A Study of Monastic Culture,* trans. C. Misrahi (New York 1962), 19–43.

Leyser, C., 'Expertise and Authority in Gregory the Great: The Social Function of *Peritia*', *Gregory the Great: A Symposium* (Notre Dame 1996), forthcoming [see Colloquia].

Lieblang, F., *Grundfragen der mystischen Theologie nach Gregors des Grossen Moralia und Ezechielhomilien* (Freiburg im Breisgau 1934).

Manselli, R., 'L'escatologismo di Gregorio Magno', *Atti del 1° Congresso internazionale di studi longobardi* (Spoleto 1952).

Manselli, R., 'L'escatologia di Gregorio Magno', *Ricerche di storia religiosa* 1 (1954), 72–88.

McCulloh, J., 'The Cult of Relics in the Letters and Dialogues of Pope Gregory the Great: A Lexicographical Study', *Traditio* 32 (1976), 145–84.

McGinn, B., 'Mystical Contemplation in Gregory the Great', *Gregory the Great: A Symposium* (Notre Dame 1996), forthcoming [see Colloquia].

Ménager, A., 'La contemplation d'après saint Grégoire le Grand', *La Vie Spirituelle* 9 (1923), 242–82.

Ménager, A., 'La contemplation d'après un Commentaire sur les Rois', *La Vie Spirituelle.* Supplément 11 (1925), 49–84.

Ménager, A., 'Les divers sens du mot "contemplatio" chez saint Grégoire le Grand', *La Vie Spirituelle.* Supplément 59 (1939), 145–169; 60 (1939), 39–56.

Sorrell, R., 'Dreams and Divination in Certain Writings of Gregory the Great', B.Litt. thesis, Oxford University (Oxford 1978).

Vogel, C., 'Deux conséquences de l'eschatologie grégorienne: La multiplication des messes privées et les moines-prêtres', *Grégoire le Grand* (Paris 1986), 267–76 [see Colloquia].

Wasselynck, R., 'La voix d'un Père de l'Église. L'orientation eschatologique de la vie chrétienne d'après S. Grégoire le Grand', *Assemblées du Seigneur,* 1 ser, vol. 2 (1962), 66–80.

Zinn, G., 'Exegesis and Spirituality in the Writings of Gregory the Great', *Gregory the Great: A Symposium* (Notre Dame 1996), forthcoming [see Colloquia].

Monasticism

Brechter, S., 'War Gregor der Grosse Abt vor seiner Erhebung zum Papst?', *Studien und Mitteilungen zur Geschichte des Benediktinerordens und seiner Zweige* 57 (1939), 209–24.

Dekkers, É., 'Saint Grégoire le Grand et les Moniales', *Collectanea Cisterciensia* 46 (1984), 23–36.

Ferrari, G., *Early Roman Monasteries: Notes for the History of the Monasteries and Convents at Rome from the V through the X Century, Studi di antichità cristiana* 23 (Rome 1957).

Gillet, R., 'Spiritualité et place du moine dans l'Église selon saint Grégoire le Grand', *Analecta Bollandiana* 83 (1961), 53–74.

Hallinger, K., 'Papst Gregor der Grosse und der Hl. Benedikt', *Regulam Sancti Benedicti,* ed. B. Steidle, Studia Anselmiana 42 (Rome 1957).

Leccisotti, T., 'Le consequenze dell'invasione longobarda per l'antico monachesimo italico', *Atti del I Congresso internazionale di studi longobardi* (Spoleto 1952).

Leccisotti, T., 'Aspetti del monachesimo in Italia', *Il monachesimo nell'alto medioevo e la formazione della civiltà occidentale* (Spoleto 1957), 331–37.

Penco, G., 'Il concetto di monaco e di vita monastica in Occidente nel secolo VI', *Studia monastica* 1 (1959), 7–50.

Porcel, O.M., *La doctrina monástica de San Gregorio Magno y la Regula monachorum* (Madrid 1950). [Also in Catholic University of America, Studies in Sacred Theology, Second Series 60].

Porcel, O.M., 'San Gregorio Magno y el monacato. Cuestiones controvertidas', *Monastica* I (1960), 1–95; Scripta et Documenta 12 (Monserrat 1960).

de Vogüé, A., 'La Règle du Maître et les Dialogues de Saint Grégoire', *Revue d'histoire ecclésiastique* 61 (1966), 44–76.

de Vogüé, A., 'Les vues de Grégoire le Grand sur la vie religieuse dans son Commentaire des Rois', *Studia monastica* 20 (1978), 17–63.

The dialogues

Boesch Gajano, S., '"Narratio" e "Expositio" nei *Dialoghi* di Gregorio Magno: tipologia dei miracoli e struttura dell'opera', *Bullettino dell'Istituto Storico Italiano per il Medioevo e Archivio Muratoriano* 88 (1979), 1–33.

Boesch Gajano, S., 'Demoni e miracoli nei *Dialoghi* di Gregorio Magno', *Hagiographie, cultures et sociétés, IVe–XIIe siècles,* Actes du Colloque organisé à Nanterre et à Paris, 2–5 Mai 1979 (Paris 1981), 263–81.

Bolton, W.F., 'The Supra-historical Sense in the *Dialogues* of Gregory the Great', *Aevum* 33 (1959), 206–13.

Cracco, G., 'Ascesa e ruolo dei *Viri Dei* nell'Italia di Gregorio Magno', *Hagiographie, cultures et sociètè, IVe–XIIe siècles* (Paris 1981), 283–97.

Cusack, P., *An Interpretation of the Second Dialogue of Gregory the Great* (Lewiston, New York 1993).

Dufner, G., *Die Dialoge Gregors des Grossen im Wandel der Zeiten und Sprachen* (Padua 1968).

Le Goff, J., '*Vita* et *Pre-exemplum* dans le 2 livre des *Dialogues* de Grégoire le Grand', *Hagiographie, cultures et sociètè, IVe–XIIe siècles* (Paris 1981), 105–20.

McCready, W., *Signs of Sanctity. Miracles in the Thought of Gregory the Great* (Toronto 1989).

Penco, G., 'Sulla struttura dialoghi dei Dialoghi di s. Gregorio', *Benedictina* 33 (1986), 329–35.

Petersen, J., *The Dialogues of Gregory the Great in Their Late Antique Cultural Background* (Toronto 1984).

Tateo, F., 'La struttura dei *Dialoghi* di Gregorio Magno', *Vetera Christianorum* 2 (1965), 101–27.

Vitale-Brovarone, A., 'La forma narrativa dei *Dialoghi* di Gregorio Magno. Problemi storico-litterari', *Atti dell'Accademia delle Scienze di Torino* 108 (1974), 95–173.

de Vogüé, A., 'La Règle du Maître et les Dialogues de saint Grégoire', *Revue d'histoire ecclésiastique* 61 (1966), 44–76.

de Vogüé, A., 'Introduction', *Grégoire le Grand, Dialogues, Sources chrétiennes* 251 (Paris 1978).

Authenticity of the dialogues

Clark, F., 'The Authenticity of Gregorian Dialogues: A Reopening of the Question?', *Grégoire le Grand* (Paris 1986), 429–44 [see Colloquia].

Clark, F., *The Pseudo-Gregorian Dialogues: A Challenge to the Traditional View,* Studies in the History of Christian Thought 37–38, 2 vols. (Leiden 1987).

Clark, F., 'St Gregory and the Enigma of the *Dialogues* : A response to Paul Meyvaert', *Journal of Ecclesiastical History* 40 (1989), 323–43.

Cremascoli, G., 'Se i *Dialogi* siano opera di Gregorio Magno: due volumi per una *vexata questio* ', *Benedictina* 36 (1989), 179–92.

Engelbert, P., 'Neue Forschungen zu den "Dialogen" Gregors des Grossen. Antworten auf Clarks These', *Erbe und Auftrag* 65 (1989), 376–93.

Gillet, R., 'Les *Dialogues* sont-ils de Grégoire?', *Revue des Études anciennes* 35 (1990), 309–74.

Godding, R., 'Les Dialogues de Grégoire le Grand. A propos d'un livre récent', *Analecta Bollandiana* 106 (1988), 201–29.

Kessler, S., 'Das Rätsel der Dialoge Gregors des Grossen', *Theologie und Philosophie* 65 (1990), 566–78.

Meyvaert, P., 'The enigma of Gregory the Great's *Dialogues*: A response to Francis Clark', *Journal of Ecclesiastical History* 39 (1988), 335–81.

Minard, P., '"Les Dialogues" de saint Grégoire et les origines du monachisme bénédictin. A propos d'un livre récent', *Revue Mabillon* 61 (1988), 471–81.

Verbraken, P.-P., '"Les Dialogues" de saint Grégoire le Grand sont-ils apocryphes? A propos d'un ouvrage récent', *Revue bénédictine* 98 (1988), 272–77.

de Vogüé, A., 'Grégoire le Grand et ses *Dialogues* d'après deux ouvrages récents', *Revue d'histoire ecclésiastiques* 83 (1988), 287–348.

de Vogüé, A., 'Les Dialogues, oeuvre authentique et publiée par Grégoire lui-même', *Gregorio Magno e il suo tempo* vol. 2 (Rome 1991), 27–40 [see Colloquia].

Liturgy

Ashworth, H., 'Gregorian Elements in the Gelasian Sacramentary', *Ephemerides liturgicae* 67 (1953), 9–23.

Ashworth, H., 'Did St Gregory the Great Compose a Sacramentary?', *Studia Patristica* 2 (1957), 3–16.

Ashworth, H., 'The Liturgical Prayers of St Gregory the Great', *Traditio* 15 (1959), 107–61.

Ashworth, H., 'Further Parallels to the "Hadrianum" from St Gregory the Great's Commentary on the First Book of Kings', *Traditio* 16 (1960), 364–73.

Deshusses, J., 'Grégoire et le Sacramentaire grégorien', *Grégoire le Grand* (Paris 1986), 637–44 [see Colloquia].

Huglo, M., 'L'Antiphonaire: archétype ou répertoire originel?, *Grégoire le Grand* (Paris 1986), 661–69 [see Colloquia].

Influence

Braga, G., 'Moralia in Job: Epitomi dei secoli VII-X e loro evoluzione', *Grégoire le Grand* (Paris 1986), 561–68 [see Colloquia].

Buddensieg, T., 'Gregory the Great, the Destroyer of Pagan Idols. The History of a Medieval Legend concerning the Decline of Ancient Art and Literature', *Journal of the Warburg and Courtauld Institutes* 28 (1965), 44–65.

The Cambridge History of the Bible, ed. G.W.H Lampe, 3 vols.; Leclercq, J., *The West from the Fathers to the Reformation,* vol. 1 (Cambridge 1976), 183–97.

Chazelle, C., 'Memory, Instruction, Worship: Gregory the Great's Influence on Early Medieval Doctrines of the Artistic', *Gregory the Great: A Symposium* (Notre Dame 1995), [see Colloquia].

Dufner, G., 'Zwei Werke Gregors des Grossen in ihrer italienischen Überlieferung', *Italia medioevale e umanistica* 6 (1963), 235–52.

Gaudemet, J., 'L'héritage de Grégoire le Grand chez les canonistes médiévaux', *Gregorio Magno e il suo temp,* vol. 2 (Rome 1991), 199–221 [see Colloquia].

Halkin, F., 'Le pape saint Grégoire le Grand dans l'hagiographie byzantine', *Recherches et documents d'hagiographie byzantine,* Subsidia hagiographica 51 (Brussels 1971), 106–11.

Kerlouégan, F., 'Grégoire le Grand et les pays celtiques', *Grégoire le Grand* (Paris 1986), 589–96, [see Colloquia].

Matter, A., 'Gregory the Great in the Twelfth Century: The *Glossa Ordinaria*', *Gregory the Great: A Symposium* (Notre Dame 1995) [see Colloquia].

Smalley, B., *The Study of the Bible in the Middle Ages* (Notre Dame 1970), 32–6.

Wasselynck, R., 'L'influence des "Moralia in Job" de saint Grégoire le Grand sur la théologie moral entre le VIIe et le XIIe siècle', Diss. Theol., 3 vols. (Lille 1956).

Wasselynck, R., 'Les compilations des Moralia in Job du VIIe au XIIe siècle', *Recherches de théologie ancienne et médiévale* 29 (1962), 5–32.

Wasselynck, R., 'Les Moralia in Job dans les ouvrages de morale du haut moyen âge latin', *Recherches de théologie ancienne et médiévale* 31 (1964), 5–31.

Wasselynck, R., 'Présence de S. Grégoire le Grand dans les recueils canoniques (Xe–XIIe s.)', *Mélanges de science religieuse* 22 (1965), 205–19.

Wasselynck, R., 'L'influence de l'exégèse de S. Grégoire le Grand sur les commentaires bibliques médiévaux (VIIe–XIIe s.)', *Recherches de théologie ancienne et médiévale* 32 (1965), 157–204.

Fredegar

AUTHORS OF THE MIDDLE AGES · 13

Historical and Religious Writers of the Latin West

Fredegar

Roger Collins

VARIORUM
1996

AUTHORS OF THE MIDDLE AGES · 13
Historical and Religious Writers of the Latin West: General Editor, Patrick J. Geary.

Published by VARIORUM
               Ashgate Publishing Limited
               Gower House, Croft Road
               Aldershot, Hants GU11 3HR
               UK

               Ashgate Publishing Company
               Old Post Road
               Brookfield, Vermont 05036
               USA

ISBN 0–86078–420–7

First published in *Authors of the Middle Ages Vol. IV, Nos. 12–13 (Historical and
Religious Writers of the Latin West)*, ed. Patrick J. Geary. Copyright © 1996 by
Variorum, Ashgate Publishing Limited. ISBN 0–86078–625–0

Typeset by Manton Typesetters,
               5–7 Eastfield Road, Louth,
               Lincolnshire LN11 7AJ

Printed and bound by Athenaeum Press. Ltd.,
Gateshead, Tyne & Wear.

CONTENTS

ABBREVIATIONS

BEC	*Bibliothèque de l'Ecole des Chartes*
CLA	Elias Avery Lowe, *Codices Latini Antiquiores* (11 volumes plus a supplement, Oxford, 1934–1971)
MGH	*Monumenta Germaniae Historica*
AA	*Auctores Antiquissimi*
SRM	*Scriptores Rerum Merovingicarum*
SRG	*Scriptores Rerum Germanicarum*
SS	*Scriptores*
NA	*Neues Archiv für ältere deutsche Geschichtskunde*
PL	*Patrologia Latina,* ed. J.P. Migne

PREFACE

However few the published pages, a study of this sort depends on the help generously and willingly supplied by specialists in the fields upon which it touches. I am greatly in the debt of Rosamond McKitterick and David Ganz for their detailed and expert replies to frequent queries relating to many of the manuscripts of the Fredegar compilations. David Ganz also kindly inspected MS Bibliothèque Nationale lat. 10910 for me, and gave his reactions to its Tironian notes, cursive marginalia and the second scribal hand. Expert advice was given by Roger Wright on the analysis of Fredegar's language, and by James Farrow on the text of Dares Phrygius. Problems in tracking down the Milan MS of Fredegar were legion, and I am most grateful to Louis Jordan III, Curator of the Ambrosiana Collection in the Medieval Institute of the University of Notre Dame for his help in trying to locate it. Especial thanks must go to Walter Goffart for actually producing the solution, and for sending me his notes on this manuscript, as well as on MS Paris Bibliothèque Nationale 4883A. I am also greatly indebted to Dr. Monika Köstlin of the Bayerische Staatsbibliothek for sending me photocopies of the late Professor Bernhard Bischoff's palaeographical notes on the Milan manuscript; also to Dr. Katerina Bierbrauer for help with the same enquiry. Tom Noble was a true facilitator, in providing introductions, not least to John Van Engen, Director of the Medieval Institute at Notre Dame, and vital e-mail addresses. One consequence of all of this has been the making of plans for a new edition of Fredegar's work, in its early Carolingian form. Research for this project was carried out at the Institute for Advanced Studies in the Humanities of the University of Edinburgh; a better and more civilized setting would be hard to imagine, for which I should like to thank its Director, Peter Jones, and his assistant, Anthea Taylor. My wife, Judith McClure, has been with me every step of the way on the long and arduous trail of the elusive 'Fredegar'. To her this work, the fruits of the chase, is dedicated.

'FREDEGAR'?

The *Chronicle of Fredegar* is remarkable for a number of reasons. Not the least of these is the fact that the work, long known by this title, may have been written by anything from one to four authors, almost certainly none of whom were named Fredegar, and was then continued nearly a century later by between two to five more authors, equally not one of whom was likely to have been so called. The name Fredegar, which is Frankish but whose use is not widely attested, probably makes its first appearance in connection with this work in 1579, with the publication in Paris of the first edition of Claude Fauchet's *Recueil des Antiquitez Gauloises et Françoises*.[1] There has been some dispute over this question, in that Bruno Krusch, who published the first modern critical edition of the text in 1888, claimed that a sixteenth-century marginal note in an eleventh-century manuscript of the work from Saint-Omer, attributing its authorship to a certain 'archdeacon Fredegar', marked the real beginning of the application of the name. He tried to devise an argument on the basis of the history of this manuscript that might link this, in his opinion, sixteenth-century note to a genuine Frankish tradition of the Carolingian period. However, Léon Levillain undermined this theory, by pointing out that Krusch had been mistaken in thinking that the first printed reference to 'Fredegar' dated from no earlier than 1598. Furthermore, he indicated that the note in the Saint-Omer manuscript was possibly written in the early seventeenth-century rather than being definitely attributable to the sixteenth. He also pointed out that Fauchet and others who employed the name in referring to the author of the chronicle never called Fredegar an archdeacon, and thus probably did not derive their knowledge from this manuscript. That the anonymous author of the note thought the author's name was Fredegar because he had read Fauchet seems, therefore, to be more probable than that Fauchet depended on the note in the Saint-Omer manuscript. However, this still leaves untouched the question of why Fauchet thought this author was called Fredegar, and to that nobody has been able to suggest an answer.[2] Although some scholars have preferred to use the more precise but

---

[1] Fauchet 1579, marginal note to Book V, chapter 1; on Fauchet see J.G. Scott, *Claude Fauchet: sa vie, son oeuvre* (Paris, 1938).

[2] Krusch 1926; Levillain 1928; Fauchet 1579 and 1599. That the 1599 edition of Fauchet is prefaced by a dedicatory epistle to King Henri IV, dated to 8 September of the same year

rather pedantic 'Pseudo-Fredegar', it is now generally accepted that convenience at least is best served by retaining the traditional name, while pointing out that it is meaningless! This is the procedure followed here. By Fredegar may be taken to mean 'the author of the compilation commonly called the *Chronicle of Fredegar*', but what that author was called by his (or her?) friends and relatives will never be known.[3] The anonymity of this author is, however, slightly less surprising, when it be appreciated that no Frankish historical writer or chronicler is known by name between the death of Gregory of Tours in 594 and the composition of Einhard's *Vita Karoli Magni* c. 825/ 30, and virtually all their works lack titles and headings in the manuscripts.

Regrettably, no evidence exists outside of his own work concerning Fredegar's identity and the details of his life; nor can testimony relating to him be found in later texts. That he lived at least part of his life in the region of Burgundy has generally been accepted on the basis of apparently detailed knowledge of and interest in aspects of its history. However, that more than one author may have been involved in the making of the compilation that goes by the name of the *Chronicle of Fredegar* inevitably complicates such arguments, and perceived changes of geographical perspective and/ or of political allegiance have been interpreted as supporting belief in multiple authorship. These arguments and the current state of the question will be considered below. What is clear, however, is that the work has not been preserved in a finished form. It terminates abruptly and inconclusively with the description of what was effectively a civil war amongst the nobility of Burgundy in 642, but the author at earlier points had alluded to events that occurred in the 650s, and at one stage promised his readers a fuller account of an episode that took place in 659 when he reached the correct chronological point in his narrative.[4] Whatever be thought of the arguments about authorship, it seems certain that the compilation was either unfinished or has lost a final section which would have taken its account from 642 to at least about 659/60. The closeness in date of the earliest manuscript, probably written in 714/5, and the now generally accepted belief that it was not the

could easily have led to the belief that this was the first printing of the work. The manuscript is Saint-Omer, Bibliothèque Municipale MS 706, on which see below p. 49 (MS 5c); the note is on f. 118r.

[3] Perhaps some psychological arguments might be advanced to suggest that the nature of the subjects preferred by Fredegar indicates that he was indeed male, but it should not be forgotten that a number of historical and hagiographic texts of this period were composed by women; see Nelson 1991. For present purposes it will be taken that Fredegar was a man, but it is not proven. The older 'Pseudo-Fredegar' is still used by Pierre Riché, *Les Carolingiens; une famille qui fit l'Europe* (Paris, 1983).

[4] Fredegar IV. 81; although serious reservations have to be expressed about the numbering by book and chapter employed by all modern editions (see below p. 8), reference in this form will be given here for greater convenience.

immediate ancestor of the other codices containing the work, might argue against the latter possibility. The crucial loss would have had to occur at a very early stage in the manuscript transmission. It has to be admitted that there can be no certainty on this question, other than for the fact that the work in practice if not in authorial intention ends where it does, and the chances of any more of it ever being found must be said to be very slight indeed.

It is also worth noting that, although internal indicators prove that the author intended to carry his narrative up to the year 659, there are no grounds for assuming that is precisely where it would have stopped. His reference to the episode in question, a successful Byzantine counter-offensive against the Arabs, in no way suggests that this was a particularly recent event from the author's perspective, let alone that it was the last thing he would have included in his narrative. All that can be said is that his work was intended to reach at least that date, thus setting one terminus for its composition. The other is provided by the date of the earliest manuscript, which has to be given as 714/5.[5] While a date of c. 660 is normally taken as the approximate time of composition or final revision of the work, the chronological possibilities must extend from 659 to 714, with some greater degree of probability lying in the earlier part of this range. In short, Fredegar could be a later rather than a mid seventh-century author.

Structure and contents of the *Chronicle*

Following the death of Gregory of Tours in 594, historical writing in the Frankish kingdoms seems to have gone into abeyance.[6] It is hard enough to know what Gregory's intentions were in writing his monumental *Ten Books of Histories*, or what audience his work reached during his lifetime, but it is clear that no one else wished either to continue his text or to emulate it by composing a comparable large-scale narrative of contemporary events in succeeding decades. In consequence, the strong if idiosyncratic light that is thrown on Frankish history of the second half of the sixth-century flickers out, to be followed by a period of almost complete gloom before a series of smaller-scale historical compositions began to be written from the 720s onwards. The only exception, and it is in its way a very significant one, to this

[5] MS Paris BN lat. 10910, on which see below pp. 40–42; Delisle 1881, 218–9, dated this manuscript to the seventh-century on paleographical grounds, putting the scribal note to one side. More recent commentators have preferred to trust the early eighth-century date: Lowe, *CLA* 608.

[6] Ganshof 1970(a), 632–42. On Gregory see most recently Martin Heinzelmann, 'Die Franken und die fränkische Geschichte in der Perspektive der Historiographie Gregors von Tours' in Scharer and Scheibelreiter 1994, 326–44.

historiographical lacuna that stretches across a 130-year period is the work now called, for reasons just discussed, the *Chronicle of Fredegar*. Problematic as it may be in many ways, it alone provides what can be known of the political history of the Frankish kingdoms between the 590s and 642. For the rest of the seventh-century recourse can only be made to the much thinner and less precise narrative of the anonymous work called the *Liber Historiae Francorum*, compiled at St Denis or possibly Soissons around the year 726/7.[7] Historical references in the handful of other texts of this period, notably a small number of contemporary saints' lives, barely compensate for the ending of the narrative provided by the *Chronicle of Fredegar*, and it is notable that problems of Merovingian regnal chronology become acute once its authority is no longer available.[8]

That the *Chronicle* is a virtually unique source does not of itself make it a necessarily reliable one. Questions have to be asked about its authorship and date, and the origins and nature of the information that it conveys. Only from the answers that can be given to such queries can any real assessment of its value be made. Hence the significance of the arguments, hinted at above, concerning the problems of single or multiple authorship, both of the main chronicle and of its eighth-century Continuations. Thus, for example, if it comes to be believed that the work was written by one author in the early 660s, what reliance can be placed on his account of events in the 590s, probably long before it could be based on first-hand knowledge? Therefore the contentious and not necessarily concluded arguments on multiple or single authorship relate directly to the question of the authority of the work as a whole or in its various parts.[9] Similar principles apply in considering the hitherto rather less controversial Continuations, which will be discussed in a separate section below.

Although normally consulted for its original contributions to the narrative history of Francia in the seventh-century, the work as a whole was clearly not intended just to provide such information. Although there are certain significant variations in the contents as found in the earliest manuscripts, it is clear that the original conception of the work was that it should take the form of a compilation of historical materials that together provided a narrative outline of human history from Adam up to the author's own times, with especial emphasis being placed in the later sections on the Frankish king-

---

[7] On this see Gerberding 1987, 146–59, who argues the case for an author working in Soissons. Nelson 1991, 160–61 speculates on the possibility of a nun of Notre Dame, Soissons, as author.

[8] On the seventh-century saints' lives see Fouracre 1990 and Wood 1988. The seventh-century chronology of *Liber Historiae Francorum* is dangerously imprecise.

[9] Goffart 1963, 232–41.

doms. This structure was preserved, but with certain important modifications being made to the individual components of the compilation, in the work of the eighth-century continuators.

The main ingredients of the original, seventh-century, compilation would seem to be as follows: an abridgement of the world chronicle known as the *Liber Generationis*, written by the Anti-pope Hippolytus (217–35) in the thirteenth year of the reign of the emperor Severus Alexander (which would be 234/5), a version of the Latin translation and continuation of the Greek chronicle of Eusebius of Caesarea (d. 338) composed by Jerome (d. 419), an abbreviated version of the chronicle of the Spanish bishop Hydatius (c. 469), a much abridged form of the first six books of Gregory of Tours' *Libri Historiarum*, extending up to 584, and possibly some at least of the chronicle of Isidore of Seville (d. 636).[10] This is far from being the full story, in that borrowings from other works, both identified and not, can also easily be detected in the compilation, especially in the first section of it. Here will be found a chronological computation entitled the *Supputatio Eusebii Hieronimi*, extending from Adam to the first (and only) year of the reign of the Austrasian Frankish king Sigibert II (613). There are also lists of popes, up to the pontificate of Theodore (642–9), and of emperors extending to the thirty first year of Heraclius (i.e. 640/1).[11] Sections of legendary stories relating both to the Ostrogothic king Theoderic (d. 526) and to the Eastern Roman emperor Justinian I (527–65) follow directly after the abridged Hydatius, and in the section of new material at the end of the work there is a substantial account of the Irish abbot Columbanus taken almost verbatim from the *Vita Columbani* of Jonas of Bobbio (written after 639).[12]

It is not easy to say with confidence what Fredegar's own contributions consisted of, as it is clear even from what little has been said so far that his method of working involved both the excerpting of existing sources and the interweaving of materials of different origins. Thus, the epitome of the first six books of Gregory's *Histories* found in this compilation clearly derives

[10] For the *Liber Generationis*, which is only otherwise found in the Codex-Calendar of 354, see Salzmann 1990, 39–42, 50–1. On the Eusebius-Jerome and Hydatius chronicles see, with references, Steven Muhlberger, *The Fifth-Century Chroniclers* (Liverpool, 1990), 8–23, and 193–266; also on Hydatius see Burgess 1993. For the various text forms of Gregory's *Historiae* first recourse should be made to Goffart 1987. For Isidore's chronicle see Collins 1994(b).

[11] The papal list gives no length for the pontificate of Theodore in MS1*, nor in the original section in MS 1, while the two MSS of Class 2 add (incorrectly) that it lasted for ten years. A later hand added the correct length of six years, one month and eighteen days to the pontificate of Theodore and extended the list of popes in MS 1 up to the sixteenth year of the pontificate of Hadrian I (i.e. 787/8); this appears in Monod's edition (pp. 24–5) but not that of Krusch.

[12] Fredegar IV. 36; cf. *Vita Columbani* 18–20, ed. Bruno Krusch, *MGH SRM* 4 (1902), 86–93; also to be found in *MGH SRG* (1905).

from an existing anonymously shortened text of those books that was circulating in Francia throughout the seventh-century.[13] However, Fredegar has not
just borrowed this; he has further condensed it and has inserted into it passages of new material not to be found in any other context, and which may
be taken to be his own work, or, more probably, as deriving from some source
or sources that were available to him but are now unknown. Fredegar's will-
ingness to make unacknowledged use of other texts is perfectly exemplified
in the employment of parts of the chapters of the *Vita Columbani* he inserted
directly into his narrative of early seventh-century Frankish history.[14] Only
the independent survival of this work makes this borrowing clear, as Fredegar
does not indicate the existence of the debt, either in the text or in the preface to the section in which it appears.

Commentators on the work have tended to pay particular attention to the
remarks made by its compiler in this preface to the final section, which covers the period from the completion of Gregory's sixth book in 584 up to the
events of 642. This section is generally regarded as representing Fredegar's
own work and his personal contribution to the collection of historical materials that he had assembled. However, as just noted, it is in this section that
the unacknowledged borrowing from the *Vita Columbani* may be found, and
there are grounds for suspecting that other undetected sources have provided
the narrative at various points throughout. The preface consists of the compiler's acknowledgement that he had hitherto drawn on the works of various
chroniclers: Jerome, Hydatius, 'a certain wise man', Isidore and Gregory (of
Tours), to bring his narrative up to the last years of the reign of the Frankish king Guntramn (561–92). On the basis of this it has been thought that
this listing of his major sources also provides the key to Fredegar's understanding of the structure of his compilation.[15] For this to work, it also has
to be argued that the 'certain wise man' referred to was the author of the
Liber Generationis, whose identity was unknown to Fredegar, and that his
place in the listing of authorities in this preface has been altered: by this
argument he should stand at the beginning of the list, in the way that the
Liber Generationis forms the first section of the work. The second then consists of Jerome's translation and continuation of Eusebius; the third comprises
the edited version of Hydatius's chronicle; part four is the abbreviated Gregory
of Tours, and part five is Fredegar's own original contribution.

---

[13] Goffart 1987, 55–76 for this condensed version of Gregory.

[14] The only other seventh-century texts referring to or showing any influence of the *Vita
Columbani* are the *Vita Wandregisili*, the *Vita Germani abbatis Grandivalliensis*, and the *Passio
Praeiecti*. See Wood 1982, 68–9; texts in Bruno Krusch (ed.), *MGH SRM* 5 (Hanover, 1910),
13–24, 33–40, and 225–48.

[15] Wallace-Hadrill edition, 1–3; see Goffart 1963, 206–16 for a resumé of the arguments
over structure.

Unfortunately, the reality of the extant manuscripts of the compilation at no point corresponds with the ideal, as apparently expressed in this preface. The chronicles of Eusebius-Jerome and of Hydatius are not distinguished by separate headings or lists of chapters in any of the manuscripts. A section of Hydatius's own introduction to his chronicle, which was an explicit continuation of that of Jerome, is preserved by Fredegar, but it is incorporated in the text, and is not given special prominence as marking a change of authorship. Even more surprising is the reference in Fredegar's preface to a debt to Isidore of Seville. The only part of the compilation that can be shown to derive directly from Isidore's chronicle is a very brief list of the events of the six days of Creation.[16] In the light of the far greater, unacknowledged debts to other sources, this reference to Isidore in Fredegar's preface to his final section is perplexing. This is all the more so if it be accepted, as it almost certainly should, that the once widely held belief that the whole of Isidore's chronicle once formed an integral part of Fredegar's compilation is quite wrong.

This argument relates to the contents of the earliest manuscript, Paris BN lat. 10910 written in 714/5 by the priest and monk Lucerius.[17] In this codex, but in none of the others containing the Fredegar collection, a version of the chronicle of Isidore of Seville, beginning with Adam and extending up to the fifth year of the reign of the emperor Heraclius and the fourth of that of the Visigothic king Sisebut (i.e. 615), follows the section of text relating to the years 584 to 642.[18] This obviously cuts across the structure and purpose of the rest of the work, by duplicating events already covered in the Eusebius-Jerome and Hydatian chronicles, as well as being chronologically out of sequence in its location in the collection. Since the time of the first critical edition, that of Bruno Krusch in 1888, it has been recognized that this component is awkwardly placed in the Paris manuscript. One of the principal French scholars to comment on the text, Maurice Baudot, argued that Isidore's chronicle had been, for whatever reason, wrongly located by the scribe of this manuscript, and should be inserted back into the main body of the compilation, probably following Hydatius and before the Gregorian epitome.[19] However, even were this to be allowed, the strange chronological leap from the fifth-century AD, the point reached in Hydatius's chronicle, all the way back to Adam and Eve at the beginning of Isidore's, remains as a problem.

[16] Krusch edition, p. 37.

[17] See below pp. 40–42 for further discussion of the date, structure and writing of MS Paris BN 10910.

[18] Mommsen, *MGH AA* XI, 399, is wrong to assert that this work also features in MSS Berne 318, Harley 5251 and Metz 134.

[19] Baudot 1928, 133–7.

The radical, but almost certainly correct, solution first proposed by Bruno Krusch and developed more recently by Walter Goffart is that the text of the chronicle of Isidore of Seville found in this manuscript does not form an integral part of the Fredegar compilation at all.[20] The Paris manuscript thus contains two separate works – the chronicles of Fredegar and of Isidore – rather than the peculiarly dismembered and redistributed components of only one. It is clear enough from Fredegar's treatment of other sources that he was quite capable of excerpting what he wanted from a source, and for all his faults is unlikely to have allowed anything as anomalous as the complete text of Isidore to break up the logical chronological development of his material that he had otherwise achieved in making the compilation. There is a further decisive, palaeographical, argument against the Isidoran chronicle as found in the Paris manuscript forming an integral part of the Fredegar compilation: some of the numerous textual errors in this part of the manuscript can be explained as the Merovingian scribe's failure to understand an exemplar in Visigothic script.[21] That his model for the Fredegar materials was a manuscript in Merovingian cursive and for the Isidore one in Visigothic minuscule makes it clear that he was drawing on two quite separate and independent sources.

Fredegar's own intentions as to the structuring of his compilation are not easy to recover. It seems clear enough that he had not intended the section of original materials relating to the period 584–642, which makes up Book Four in all modern editions, to be divided up into chapters. The text itself presents an obvious chronological structuring by the regnal years of a number of named Merovingian kings. This has actually been disturbed by the dividing up of the contents into chapters. In some cases the events of a single year are split between one or more chapters, and in others one chapter embraces two years. Decisively, the chapter numbers in the earliest manuscript appear to have been added by a later hand, probably indicating that they were taken from another manuscript of the work and did not form part an integral part of it when Lucerius was writing his codex in 714/5.

The division of the compilation into books is more problematic, and in large measure derives from decisions taken somewhat arbitrarily by Bruno Krusch when preparing his 1888 edition. The Paris manuscript does not use the term 'Book' for its divisions of the contents, and its scribe may have seen them instead as being separate chronicles. A note on folio 1v, now only visible under ultraviolet light, indicates that the heading for the first section referred to it as 'The First Chronicle'.[22] Lucerius may indeed have regarded

---

[20] Goffart 1963, 207–16.

[21] Beeson 1913, 73; for the probable Merovingian cursive model for the rest of the manuscript see Wallace-Hadrill edition, xlviii.

[22] Goffart 1963, 209–10, note 13.

the compilation not as a single work, but as a collection of discrete chronicles. Such a view is reinforced by his treatment of the final section, consisting primarily of what is normally seen as Fredegar's own original composition. This is prefaced by the heading *Prologus cuiusdam sapientis,* 'Prologue of a certain wise man'. Lucerius obviously did not know to whom to attribute responsibility for this section, and took the phrase 'a certain wise man' from the preface to this part of the compilation. He clearly did not regard this section as being the work of the original compiler; apparently seeing it merely as another chronicle, though in this case an anonymous one.

It is only with the manuscripts of Classes Two and Three that references to a division by 'Book' start to appear in the text.[23] However, the evidence is far from clear or consistent. The two manuscripts of Class Two call the Gregory epitome 'Book Four', and the section of new material relating to 584–642 appears to constitute 'Book Five'. The *Liber Generationis* and its attendant lists also figure as the explicit contents of Book One. However, no heading can be found for a Book Three, and all of the chapters of the intervening sections from Jerome, Hydatius and the Theoderic-Justinian legends are listed together, without a book heading, immediately after the conclusion of Book One.[24] In the manuscripts of Class Three an attempt is made to rationalise this by inserting a new text, the *De Cursu Temporum* of the African bishop Quintus Julius Hilarian (c. 397 AD), between the Jerome/Hydatius/legends collection and the epitome of Gregory of Tours.[25] This, thus, seems to provide the contents of a Book Three. However, no such heading was used in any of the manuscripts of this class, any more than it had been in those of Class Two. It seems possible to suppose that at an early point in the manuscript transmission, someone tried to impose a five-book structure on the work, which for some reason has only partially survived in the manuscript tradition.

The only practical solution to this problem would seem to be to accept the probable existence of a division in the collection between on the one hand the Eusebius-Jerome chronicle and on the other the chronicle of Hydatius and the legends relating to Theoderic, Justinian and Belisarius. This would not

[23] For the manuscript classes see pp. 39–49 below. Classes Four and Five do not concern us here, as they represent two later stages of revision or re-use of the material. The manuscripts of Classes Two and Three are all that survive as evidence of the intermediate stages between Fredegar and Lucerius on the one hand and the making of the revised version of 751/768, which was clearly organized around a three-book structure.

[24] MS London, British Library Harley 5251 demonstrates these divisions and headings on folios 62v, 89r, 1r and 20r–21r respectively.

[25] The absence of this work from Lucerius's manuscript, Paris BN 10910, as well as from the Class Two manuscripts, would indicate that this could not have formed a part of Fredegar's own compilation.

only provide a logical point at which to insert the break between the second and third books, but is hinted at by what remains of the heading to the section following Book One. Thus, for example, in the manuscripts of Class Two will be found the rubric *INCIPIUNT CAPITULA CHRONICI HIERONYMI EXCARPSUM*. This would imply that the intended contents of the section following the *Liber Generationis* would have been Jerome's Latin translation and continuation of Eusebius. This should have been 'Book Two'. The rubric in the same class of manuscripts immediately preceding the preface to the epitome of Gregory of Tours, which here explicitly constitutes Book Four, reads *EXPLICIT LIBER TERTIUS*. That such a third book would have had to incorporate the materials now interposed between Jerome's chronicle and the epitome of Gregory is self-evident.

It is striking that all of the manuscripts of the first three classes share the problem of the lack of clear division between the chronicles of Jerome and of Hydatius, while retaining Hydatius's preface, and at the same time those of Classes Two and Three have the problem of a lack of clear delineation of the second and third books of the collection. This common difficulty found in the two strands of the manuscript tradition from the earliest periods leads to the conclusion that the failure to mark clearly the division between Jerome's work and that of Hydatius was a feature of the archetype from which all three classes of manuscripts ultimately derived. If that be accepted, it also makes it very probable that it was Fredegar himself who first used a five-book structure. If not, it is peculiar that whoever did subsequently impose such an organization of the material ran into a difficulty over the contents of his second and third books, which can only be explained by reference to a feature also common to MS Paris BN 10910, the only manuscript not to use a division by book. In other words, a more or less rational scribe trying subsequently to impose a book structure on the Paris manuscript or its equivalent would have chosen to use a four-part division, representing the explicit breaks in the contents that can be seen in that codex. It is thus possible that Lucerius, the scribe of the Paris manuscript, omitted a set of incomplete and confusing book headings to be found in his model, which, however, were to be preserved in the other branch of the manuscript tradition. If this be allowed, the loss of the proper headings for Books Two and Three and the confusion over the division between Jerome and Hydatius may be yet other symptoms of the incomplete nature of Fredegar's autograph manuscript, from which all subsequent copies ultimately derived.

Unfortunately for twentieth-century students of Fredegar, Bruno Krusch ignored this possibility and imposed a four-book structure on the work, which does not correspond with that to be found in any of the manuscripts. He was convinced that to Fredegar the chronicles of Jerome and Hydatius formed but a single book. He was right to assume that Fredegar received these two works as part of a single corpus, as has been shown by Richard Burgess's study of the manuscript tradition of Hydatius.[26] However, this corpus also included the *Liber Generationis*, which Fredegar never had any problem in distinguishing from other texts. On the basis of his assumption, Krusch labelled the *Liber Generationis* and its lists 'Book One', and the Gregory epitome 'Book Three', leaving all of the intervening material to make up 'Book Two'. Fredegar's section on the years 584–642 thus came to be called 'Book Four'. Although contradicting the specific headings in the manuscripts of Classes Two and Three and imposing an alien terminology on that of Class One, this structure was retained in the two subsequent editions of Wallace-Hadrill and Kusternig, and is that used for reference in all scholarly publication that makes use of Fredegar's work. Convenient or necessary as it may be to make use of it here, it must be stressed that it does not represent anything of the way that Fredegar himself will have thought of his collection.

A genuinely eighth-century development of the structure of the compilation was the reorganization of the contents into three books, which formed part of the process of revision and enlargement carried out in 751. The anonymous continuator, working under the instructions of Count Childebrand, a half-brother of Charles Martel, not only added several sections of new material, but also replaced the *Liber Generationis*, which had hitherto formed Book One of the compilation with Hilarian's *De Cursu Temporum*, and combined this with the abbreviated chronicles of Jerome and Hydatius to make up a new and much larger first book. The second book of the revised version comprised the epitome of Gregory of Tours, and a third book was made up of the 'original' final sections of Fredegar, together with the Continuations up to the year 751. The work in this three-book structure received a further continuation, bringing its account up to 768.[27] The intentions behind these eighth-century continuations and the attendant restructuring of the seventh-century compilation will be considered in a separate section below.

One author or many?

The detailed and contentious arguments over the stages of composition of the collection need to be reviewed here, as the debate over single versus multiple authorship has reached something of a state of impasse, without a full and general agreement on the solution having been reached. Lacking some view on this, the problems of the authority of all or any part of the work that were mentioned above cannot be settled. For Bruno Krusch, the first modern editor of the work, the making of the compilation in the form we

---

[26] Burgess 1993, 12. His assumption that this collection had to have arrived in Gaul by 613 is based on misplaced trust in Krusch's views on multiple authorship.

[27] Collins 1994(a), 241–6.

now have it was attributable to the activities of three or possibly four separate contributors. The first of these, whom he held had to be working around
the year 613, put together the basic collection of texts, comprising the *Liber
Generationis*, the chronicles of Jerome-Eusebius and of Hydatius, and the
legendary tales about Theoderic and Justinian. To these texts this first author,
whom Krusch designated 'A', added a short chronicle of his own composition, covering the years 584 to 613. Then in 642 a quite different person,
author 'B', made the abridgement of the first six books of the *Histories* of
Gregory of Tours, to which he added another original chronicle covering the
years 614–41, and added both of these to the collection made in 613. Subsequently, around the year 660, yet a third contributor ('C') took his pred-
ecessors' composite work, and interpolated various sections of new material
into it, particularly relating to events outside Francia, but including some
sections on internal events that had a more pronouncedly pro-Austrasian character than the rest of the text. Krusch was prepared to contemplate the possibility that the author of the Austrasian interpolated materials, which form
chapters 81–2, 85–8 and probably chapter 48 of book IV in his edition, was
not the same man as the overall reviser of the text working c. 660 and who
contributed the sections of non-Frankish stories (and who is thus a possible
'D'), but he preferred to believe in three rather than four authors, and amal-
gamated his hypothetical 'D' with 'C'. He also thought on the basis of internal indicators in the contents of the text that the compiler of 613 and the
writer working in 642 were probably Burgundians from Avenches, while the
interpolator-editor of c. 660 was an Austrasian who was most likely to have
lived in Metz.[28]

All of this complex argument was in contrast to the previous unquestioned
assurance that the whole compilation was the work of a single individual.
Gabriel Monod, who published a diplomatic edition of the oldest extant
manuscript in 1898, noted Krusch's arguments but dismissed them in favour
of a restatement of traditional belief in a single author. He was, though, as
confident as Krusch that he could delineate the salient characteristics of
'Fredegar', whom he characterized as 'a monk of Gallo-Roman origin, living at Saint-Marcel in Chalon-sur-Saône, who wrote his chronicle around 642,
and later on, between 658 and 664, added various extra touches to his
work.'[29] A disciple of Krusch, Gustav Schnürer developed the arguments
about multiple authorship yet further in a book published in 1900, in which

---

[28] Krusch 1882, 423–55.

[29] Monod (edition), 12–13, and n. 1. Fustel de Coulanges 1888, 7–8, commenting on an
earlier presentation of this idea in Monod 1878(b), was very critical of the idea that Fredegar
was a monk, or any form of cleric. Kusternig edition, 12, following in this tradition, draws
attention to the legal and administrative terminology and phraseology to be found in various
parts of the work.

he argued that the first compiler was working in 616 rather than 613. He chose this date because he interpreted a reference in the preface to the final book as implying that the work was composed after the ending of the independent kingdom of Burgundy, which he saw as being brought about at the assembly held at Bonneuil in 616.[30] He also tried to further divide up the contents of the section of new material between the various contributors, and to deduce the existence and nature of hitherto undetected sources. Thus, he recognized that the first contributor appeared to be both highly prejudiced against queen Brunechildis (d. 613) and yet at the same time an enthusiastic supporter of her grandson and protégé the Burgundian king Theuderic II (596–613). This he explained by hypothesizing the existence of an otherwise unknown work on 'The Wars of Theuderic', written by a Burgundian author who supported Brunechildis, which the compiler of 616 then used, without recognizing that aspects of its narrative were at variance with his own feelings of hostility towards that queen. Schnürer also tried his hand at depicting or even unmasking the anonymous authors. Believing that the first compiler, Krusch's 'A', had been close to the Burgundian court in the time of Theuderic II and had also proved unusually well informed about the monastery of Luxeuil, he thought that he could identify him as Agrestius, a royal notary who became a monk of Luxeuil after 613. The second author, working around 642, he could not put a name to, but he underlined some of his salient characteristics and argued that he was in origin a Burgundian, who had some connection with Flaochad (d. 642) the Mayor of the Palace in Burgundy, but was actually writing in an unidentifiable location further to the south.[31]

In 1902 Louis Halphen published a review of Schnürer's book rightly criticizing him for his over-imaginative reconstruction, which had involved positing a large number of interpolations in the text, some quite minute in size. However, Halphen did accept Schnürer's view that the destruction of the Burgundian kingdom had not taken place by the point (Book Four chapter 39 in Krusch's and all subsequent editions) at which Krusch believed the first author stopped writing. He thus accepted Schnürer's contention that the date of composition must be later than 613, but rejected the divide that the latter made at Book Four chapter 44 (in 616) in favour of one that he thought he detected at the end of chapter 42 (therefore in 614), since he saw the destruction of Burgundy referred to in the preface as occurring with the overthrow of Sigibert II in 613 rather than with the Council of Bonneuil. He also

---

[30] For this see Fredegar IV. 44: Wallace-Hadrill edition, 37. No *acta* of this assembly are known for certain, but the mutilated text to be found in MS Berlin Deutsche Staatsbibliothek Philipps 1743, folio 300v, would be a possible candidate.

[31] Schnürer 1900.

poured scorn on Schnürer's attempted identification of the first two of the three authors, but did not question the threefold division of authorship first advanced by Krusch.[32]

The arguments for single authorship were powerfully revived by the great French historian of Late Antiquity and the Early Middle Ages, Ferdinand Lot who, among other things, was a devoted pupil of Gabriel Monod. In an article published in 1914 he reviewed the various arguments previously advanced, and effectively undermined the need for believing in the existence of an earlier author working in the 613/6 period. He saw the first two of Krusch's authors, his 'A' and 'B', as being the same man, putting together the whole compilation at some point after 642. Lot did, however, accept that a revision of the work took place around the year 660, and that this might have been done by somebody other than the original author. In other words he was prepared at least in theory to accept the possibility of the existence of Krusch's author 'C'. He was also willing to regard chapters 48, 81–2 and 84 of the final section as being interpolations. Neither at this point nor subsequently was Krusch prepared to compromise on his three-author structure and riposted briefly in a two-page review of Lot's article later in the same year.[33] The coming of the First World War put a temporary halt to these hostilities, which were not to be resumed until the late 1920s.

In 1928 Maurice Baudot, accepting and extending Lot's case for a single author, made a new attempt to identify the real Fredegar. He argued that the quantity and variety of the information in the section of new material for the years 584–642 indicated that the compiler was a royal official, and the apparent variety of geographical perspectives he offered, a feature underlined by Schnürer, was a reflection of the way that he moved around with the court. Furthermore, Baudot felt that the both the Transjuran region and its count Berthar received a disproportionate prominence in the later parts of the narrative, and this led him to attribute the authorship to this very Berthar, whom he felt was thus providing eyewitness testimony to the events described from 604 onwards. This surprising longevity, for a final revision of the work around 660 could not be denied, together with other weaknesses in his arguments laid Baudot open to damning criticisms.[34]

Other features of Baudot's article were more significant than his attempted identification of Fredegar with Count Berthar, but they tended to be overlooked in the general disapprobation of his authorial claims. In particular he had attacked the interpretation of the phrase in the Preface to Book Four, which had been used by Krusch, Schnürer and Halphen as the mainstay for

[32] Halphen 1902.
[33] Lot 1914; Krusch 1914.
[34] Baudot 1928, 162–70; Goffart 1963, 347–51.

their common belief that a first author had been writing in the period 613/6. This required the phrase in the preface '*usque regnum Guntchramni decedentem*' – 'until the end (or decline) of the kingdom (or reign) of Guntramn' – to imply 'the ending of Guntramn's kingdom', in other words of an independent realm of Burgundy.[35] Baudot insisted, surely correctly, that both the language and the context of the phrase required it to be taken literally, as just referring chronologically to the latter part of the reign of Guntramn. The transition from the material in the abbreviated Gregory of Tours to the new section of text composed by Fredegar occurred in the description of the events of the year 584. The period 584–92 could indeed be seen as the final or declining part of a reign that lasted from 561 to 592.

In 1926 in a published lecture, Krusch returned to the fray with a consideration of the origin of the pseudonym Fredegar and a general restatement of his views, now nearly fifty years old, on the composition and authorial structure of the chronicle. This was reviewed in 1928 by the great French historian and textual scholar Léon Levillain, who provided a short but powerful presentation of the arguments in favour of single authorship, supporting not least Baudot's position on the interpretation of the '*regnum Guntechramni*' phrase. He rejected the tentative compromise that Lot had been willing to make, in accepting the existence of a possible separate reviser working around 660 on a compilation initially made after 642. As Levillain saw it 'the Chronicle of Fredegar is the work of a single author, a Burgundian originating in the region of Avenches, who undertook the writing of the history of his own times in the context of a universal chronicle between 658 and 661'. He also agreed with Lot (and Fustel de Coulanges) that this author was 'a layman and frequenter of royal courts; thus most probably a grandee'.[36]

In 1934 Krusch, in his final contribution to the debate he had initiated, made a short attempt to counter the criticisms made by Levillain. However, the same year saw the publication of an article which moved the discussion onto a new plane and gave renewed if altered force to the arguments for multiple authorship, which had remained almost an article of faith for German scholars since 1882. This was the contribution of a new participant, Siegmund Hellmann, whose linguistic analysis of much of Book Four seemed to provide powerful philological support for a modified version of Krusch's original position. Where Hellmann differed was in showing that the Austrasian elements in the work were less distinctive than had previously been believed, and that it was therefore possible to dispense with Krusch's third author, and to settle for two Burgundians, one writing around 614 and the other about 660. He thus saw the 'real' Fredegar, who actually compiled the whole col-

---

[35] Krusch edition, 123; Wallace-Hadrill edition, 1.
[36] Krusch 1926; Levillain 1928, 94–5 for the quotation.

lection, as the latter. His predecessor of c. 614 was the author of a set of Burgundian annals, covering the years 584 to 614, which came to be incorporated into the compilation made c. 660.[37] Hellmann's linguistic arguments were also so trenchantly technical that he effectively cleared the field of all historians of an opposing cast of mind, as they were unable to take him on his own ground. In consequence the Hellmann two-author theory was to remain unchallenged for several decades. It was accepted by Michael Wallace-Hadrill in his edition of the final section of the chronicle, published in 1960, and was endorsed by the Flemish historian François Louis Ganshof in a booklet he published on Fredegar in 1970.[38]

By that time, however, the question had once more been forcefully reopened, for the first time in nearly thirty years. This was thanks to the publication of an article by Walter Goffart in 1963. Despite the long ascendancy of Hellmann's modification of Krusch's view, Goffart laid down the gauntlet by proclaiming that 'the burden of proof rests upon those who challenge the idea of single authorship, and if their attempts fail, the presumption must be that Fredegar is one man'. He attacked the arguments that had been used to suggest a change in the character and quality of the chronicle after 613/4 and thus the presence of two separate compositions. He also settled the question of the role of the chronicle of Isidore, here supporting and indeed proving the validity of Krusch's contention that this was not an integral part of the compilation, despite its appearance in the earliest manuscript.[39]

The only area in which Goffart felt himself inadequately equipped to tackle Hellmann was in the matter of the linguistic analysis that seemingly supported dual authorship. Here help was on the way, in the form of Alvar Erikson's article published in Sweden in 1965. Erikson undermined Hellmann's philological arguments, allowing only some slight indications of stylistic variety, best explained by the presence of undigested source material in the section of text he had analysed.[40] The joint but independent assaults of Goffart and Erikson on the previously dominant dual authorship theory of Hellmann have undermined its credibility, if not quite killed it off.[41] Kusternig's 1982 edition accepted single authorship, but explicit belief in 'at least two Fredegar authors' was restated as recently as 1987.[42]

---

[37] Krusch 1934; Hellmann 1934.

[38] Wallace-Hadrill edition, xix–xxiv; Ganshof 1970(b), 7–8.

[39] Goffart 1963.

[40] Erikson 1965.

[41] It is possible that Wallace-Hadrill himself came implicitly to accept the theory of single authorship, as references to Fredegar in his *The Frankish Church* (Oxford, 1983), 55, 58, 70, 83 etc. treat him as a single individual.

[42] Gerberding 1987, 14, based on the existence of two slightly varied versions of the origin story of the Franks in different parts of the compilation.

Fredegar's sources

A desire to get at what is wholly 'new' and original in Fredegar's compilation has led to particular concentration of scholarly attention on the final
section of the work, a tendency accentuated by the self-imposed limits of the
Wallace-Hadrill edition, which confines itself to 'Book Four' (i.e. the material relating to the period 584–642) and the Continuations. This has resulted
in some neglect both of Fredegar's own contributions to earlier sections of
his collection and to wider questions of the origin and nature of his sources.
These latter in particular may help to throw some light on the problems of
his own identity, location and intentions. Analysis of his text reveals something of the wealth of materials that he had at his disposal, to which he makes
no overt reference, but which contributed significantly to his work. These
included the *Vita Columbani*, written by Jonas a monk of Bobbio. Fredegar's
unacknowledged use of a substantial extract of this both constitutes the earliest testimony to the dissemination of this work, and considerably predates
the earliest extant manuscript of it.[43] It also might provide a further slender
clue as to his area of work and interests.

Jonas wrote his account of Columbanus (d. 615), the Irish abbot who
founded both the monastery of Luxeuil in Burgundy (c. 595) and that of
Bobbio (613) in north-eastern Italy, after the death in 639 of abbot Bertulf
of Bobbio. It was dedicated to the latter's successor Bobolenus and to abbot Waldelenus of Luxeuil (629–70). Its date of completion cannot easily
be gauged. It has been thought that it must be earlier than 643, as Jonas
is not himself described as being an abbot, and it has been claimed that
he should be identified with the 'Jonatus' who became abbot of
Marchiennes, near Saint-Amand, in that year. However, the grounds for
making such an identification are woefully thin. Fredegar, at work no earlier than c. 659, is the first real *terminus post quem non* for the composition of the *Vita Columbani*. The subject of the work and its dedication
would imply that its earliest dissemination would have been from Bobbio
and Luxeuil, and this suggests both that Fredegar was in contact with one
or other of these, and that he was fundamentally in sympathy with
Columbanian monasticism. It is not, however, necessary to assume that he
was himself a monk, as a number of prominent laymen became attracted
to the new wave of Irish monastic practices that swept over many parts of
Francia in the seventh-century.[44]

---

[43] Metz, Grand Séminaire, MS 1, assigned to the later ninth-century. This MS was unknown
to Krusch who based his 1902 *MGH SRM* IV edition of the *Vita Columbani* on the early tenth-
century St Gall MS 553; see Leclercq 1955.

[44] Prinz (1988), 124–85.

Other substantial sections of the central part of Fredegar's compilation are formed from a series of stories relating to non-Frankish figures, notably the Ostrogothic king Theoderic (493–526) and the Eastern Roman emperor Justinian I (527–65) and his general Belisarius. There is also a short section on the Alamannic king Chrocus lodged between the Theoderic and Justinian sections.[45] All of this follows the epitome of Hydatius's chronicle and precedes that of the first six books of Gregory's *Libri Decem Historiarum*. This material has largely been ignored, and certainly not taken very seriously in the discussion of the structuring of the compilation, largely because of its legendary and non-historical nature. In quantity it exceeds the *Liber Generationis* and it could be argued, both from its size and the order of names in the much discussed preface to the final book, that it was to the author of this group of tales that Fredegar was referring when he described himself as using the work 'of a certain wise man'.

While the demonstrably legendary character of this material may appear to distance it from the more obviously historical records that make up the rest of the work that Fredegar selected from other authors or composed himself, its inclusion is further testimony to his love of a good story. Not for Fredegar were the kind of concerns later to be expressed by Bede in the preface to his *Ecclesiastical History*, as to how the authenticity of his account could be guaranteed. Fredegar liked a good tale, and would include it if it appealed to him, however far-fetched the subject. This was certainly a matter of choice on his part, and not the desperation of a compiler hunting around for any information he could lay his hands on. Comparison of both Fredegar's text of the works of Hydatius and of Gregory of Tours with their authors' own original versions or with other epitomes of them shows just how selective he could be. There was much that was available to him by way of sound historical material that just did not interest him.

Most of what is to be found in Fredegar's interpolations and in his own final section of new material cannot be paralleled elsewhere. His sources may in some cases be verbal, in others such as the stories about Theoderic and Justinian, which will be considered below, they were almost certainly written. All too often those sources, while their existence may easily be deduced, have neither survived themselves nor made any impact on the work of others. It is therefore interesting to examine a case in which Fredegar provides an account which can be compared with other versions of the same event. His report of the tribulations and eventual murder of bishop Desiderius of Vienne can be taken in conjunction with that of the *Vita Desiderii* almost certainly written by the Visigothic king Sisebut (611/12–20), and with that of an anonymous and probably early seventh-century account of the bishop's

---

[45] On this section see Demougeot 1962 and Drinkwater 1987.

life and passion from Vienne.[46] Although Fredegar's version of the story of bishop Desiderius's exile, recall and subsequent killing is very brief in comparison with the hagiographic texts, he not only provides a chronology that they lack but also offers additional information. The deposition of Desiderius was carried out in 603/4 by a synod held at Chalon, at the instigation not just of queen Brunechildis but also of bishop Aridius of Lyon. In 607/8 he returned from exile but was subsequently stoned to death on the orders of king Theuderic II, again acting on the advice of Brunechildis and bishop Aridius.[47] It is only Fredegar who is able to locate the synod at Chalon-sur Saône, who provides dating for some of these events via the regnal chronology of Theuderic II, and who mentions the close involvement of bishop Aridius. None of these features contradicts the longer but less specific accounts of the Visigothic and Frankish hagiographic texts, but complements them, and testifies both to Fredegar's independence and the precision of some of his information.

Particularly notable in the final section of the compilation are the numerous reports of events that occurred beyond the frontiers of Francia. These relate to Spain, Italy and the Eastern Roman or Byzantine empire. Using for convenience the book and chapter divisions found in the modern editions, it can be noted that of the ninety chapters of Book Four, seven relate to Spanish affairs, ten to Italian, and eight to Byzantine.[48] None refer to events in the British Isles. A number of the episodes described concern what may be termed diplomatic relations, such as the short-lived betrothal in 607 of the Visigothic princess Ermenberga to Theuderic II of Burgundy, and are seen from what was clearly a Frankish perspective. Others, however, have no Frankish dimension, and thus must represent information that reached Fredegar from outside his own land. The Spanish reports tend, not very surprisingly, to be concerned with royal successions; though Fredegar could pick up interesting incidental details, such as the advanced age of king Chindasuinth (642–53), who was said to be ninety at the time of his death. Some of his Spanish information, notably Sisebut's expulsion of Frankish forces from Cantabria, has been derided, but it may actually deserve more confidence than it has been shown.[49]

---

[46] Fredegar IV. 24 and 32; Juan Gil (ed.), *Vita Desiderii* in *idem, Miscellanea Wisigothica* (Seville, 1972), 52–68; Fontaine 1980; Bruno Krusch (ed.), *Passio Desiderii, MGH SRM* 3, 638–45; on which see Wood 1982, 70–1.

[47] Wood 1988, 373–5, argues that the date of the execution should be c. 611. The differences in their accounts might negate his suggestion (Wood 1994, 248) that Fredegar had read Sisebut's *Vita Desiderii*.

[48] Fredegar IV. chs. 6, 8, 30–1, 33, 73 and 82 (Spanish); 13, 31, 34, 45, 49–51, 69–71 (Italian); 9, 11, 23, 63–6, 81 (Byzantine).

[49] Wallace-Hadrill edition, 21 with n.3; for a defence of Fredegar here see Collins 1986, 91–3.

More interesting still is Fredegar's Italian information. For the narrative history of the Lombard kingdom in Italy recourse is normally made to the *Historia Langobardorum* of Paul the Deacon, written at Monte Cassino in the 790s, which in turn relied on earlier lost works such as that of bishop Secundus of Trento (d. 612). However, Paul's account becomes extremely thin once deprived of the latter's support. For the 620s and 630s, and in particular the reign of Arioald (626–36) and the early part of that of Rothari (636–52), it is Fredegar, whose work was almost certainly unknown to Paul, who can provide the most substantial references to political events in Italy, albeit in the form of dramatic tales rather than plain narrative.[50]

Fredegar's Byzantine information is of two kinds. There are a number of direct references to military and political events, the authenticity of which can be confirmed by other sources, and there are also a small number of clearly legendary tales, very similar in character to those concerning Theoderic, Belisarius and Justinian to be found in an earlier part of the work. These include the tale of the conversion to Christianity of the wife of the Shah of Iran, and the single combat of the emperor Heraclius and a Persian noble.[51] The excessive concern of modern commentators with the book structuring of the compilation has served to obfuscate the clear generic and stylistic links between the section of materials on these sixth-century figures, inserted after the epitome of the chronicle of Hydatius, and the seventh-century stories located in the 'original' section of Fredegar's collection. It is quite reasonable to assume that all of these legendary pieces came from a single source, broken up and distributed by Fredegar throughout his work in more or less the right chronological location. One of these Byzantine stories, recounting how 'Caesara' the wife of the Persian ruler 'Anlauf' came secretly to Constantinople to be baptised in the time of the emperor Maurice (582–602), and how when Sassanian ambassadors came to find her she only agreed to return to her husband if he too became a Christian, also appears in the *History of the Lombards* of Paul the Deacon.[52] Paul's version is a little briefer than that of Fredegar and omits some of the characters to be found in the latter's account. It is, however, similar in outline, calls the queen 'Caesara' though without naming her husband, and concludes with the latter and 60,000 of his subjects receiving baptism. Where Paul does diverge from Fredegar is in locating the episode in the reign of Constans II (642–68) rather than that of Maurice. This difference and the fact that Paul was clearly ignorant of

[50] Ludwig Bethmann, 'Paulus Diaconus, seiner Leben und Schriften', *Archiv*, 10 (1851), 247–334; also see Monod 1879. It is inconceivable that Paul would not have used Fredegar's Italian material when his own information on this period was so limited. Nor would the literary character of Fredegar's stories have been out of keeping with the rest of Paul's narrative.

[51] Fredegar IV. 9 and 64.

[52] Paul, *Historia Langobardorum* IV. 50, ed. G. Waitz, *MGH SRG* (Hanover, 1890), 173.

the otherwise useful Italian stories in Fredegar indicates that the latter's work was not the source of his information. A version of the tale must, therefore, have been circulating independently in later eighth-century Italy.

This leads to the possibility that these legendary tales concerning Byzantine and Italian affairs came to Fredegar from Italy. It has been suggested that the stories about Belisarius found in Fredegar originated in the Eastern Roman Empire, but there are no good reasons for separating these off from the later tales of the times of Maurice and Heraclius.[53] If all of these were first devised in the East they would have been written in Greek, and to have appeared in a version comprehensible to Fredegar would need to have been given a Latin translation in one of the few Latin-speaking parts of the Empire. Of these the Byzantine enclave in Italy would seem the most likely candidate. It is equally possible that it was in Lombard Italy that they actually originated.

Some of Fredegar's Byzantine information was more historical than legendary, if not always accurate in all its details. Thus he correctly reported Phocas's overthrowing of the emperor Maurice in 602, but has him coming from the Persian rather than the Danube frontier.[54] The account of the successful revolt against Phocas in 610 contains a number of genuine elements, but conflates the successful rebel Heraclius with his father, and makes the senators overthrow Phocas because he had thrown the imperial treasure into the sea as a gift to Neptune. The chronological location of this episode is also uneasy: it is inserted at a point equivalent to events in Francia in 629, but serves as the prelude to a series of narratives concerning the whole of Heraclius's reign (610–41). In outline these record his wars against first the Persians and then the Arabs, but are imprecise and exaggerated in their details. On the other hand, Fredegar knew accurately enough that in his last years Heraclius married his niece and was regarded as a heretic, at least in western eyes. It is thus unlikely that Fredegar was receiving information on these events directly from Byzantium. Again, an Italian source, distorting information not very fully reported or well understood, might help explain these features in his narrative. Interestingly, the brief synopsis he gives of the reign of his own contemporary, the emperor Constans II (642–68) seems both more accurate and more precise. He promised to give more details at a later stage in the work, particularly about the emperor's renewal of war against the Arabs in 658/9, but this would have appeared in the part that was either never written or has been lost.

---

[53] Salmon 1929/30.

[54] On this episode see Michael Whitby, *The Emperor Maurice and his Historian* (Oxford, 1988), 24–7.

It should not be assumed that Fredegar's use of earlier sources was un-critical or simplistic. For example, in the epitome of the first six books of Gregory of Tours he twice adds the information that the Visigothic king Amalaric (526–31) was killed in Barcelona.[55] Although Gregory reports the king's death with considerable circumstantial detail, he never mentioned where it occurred. The anonymous author of the *Liber Historiae Francorum*, writ-ing around 726/7, merely paraphrased Gregory. Of Frankish authors only Fredegar records this location. Among other sources for this event, neither Jordanes nor Procopius, both writing in the mid-sixth-century, mention Bar-celona. Isidore of Seville does not mention the episode in his chronicle, but in his *Historia Gothorum* of 625/6 reports that Amalaric was killed in Bar-celona, but attributed responsibility to the king's own supporters. Only the short sixth-century *Chronicon Caesaraugustanae* joins Fredegar in locating the event in Barcelona and making the Franks responsible.[56]

Particularly striking are the additions made to Gregory by Fredegar relat-ing to the origins and early history of the Franks. This is where the story of the supernatural genesis of the Merovingian dynasty, through the union of the wife of king Chlodio with 'a creature of Neptune similar to a Quinotaur' may be found, and also the first reference to the Trojan origins of the Franks themselves, leading not least to their founding a new city of Troy on the banks of the Rhine.[57] Whether Fredegar was himself the source for such tales, or whether he was recording legendary accounts that were starting to gain currency more widely in seventh-century Francia cannot be determined. He certainly did not invent the theme of Trojan origins, which can be found prefigured in the report of Trojans settling in Gaul in the work of the fourth-century Roman historian Ammianus Marcellinus.[58] It also appears independ-ently in the early eighth-century *Liber Historiae Francorum*. The pseudony-mous *Fall of Troy* of 'Dares the Phrygian', was also circulating in Francia in the time of Fredegar, and in the mid-eighth-century the earliest known version of it became incorporated into his compilation as a constituent of the revised version associated with the Continuations.

Fredegar also inserted into Gregory's stories such brief additional details as the name of Childeric's friend, who advised him when to return from exile among the Thuringians. It is possible that such additions are little more than the mark of a storyteller's wish to add verisimilitude to his narrative, but may

[55] Fredegar III. 30 and 41; ed. Krusch, 103 and 105.

[56] *Chronicorum Caesaraugustanorum Reliquiae*, ed. T. Mommsen, *MGH AA*, 11 (Berlin, 1894), 223; on this see Collins 1994(b), 355–7.

[57] Krusch's edition III. 9 and III. 21, pp. 95 and 93; Krusch, 93 n.3, thought the city story referred to Xanten.

[58] Ammianus Marcellinus, XV. ix. 5; see Wallace-Hadrill 1957/8, 79–83, and Gerberding 1987, 13–19.

represent a wider process of the accumulation of oral traditions, not necessarily of any historical worth, around Gregory's text.[59] Certainly Fredegar
loved a good story. He augmented Gregory's brief statement about the sack
of Trier by the Franks with a tale of how a Roman senator called Lucius
betrayed the city out of a desire for revenge on the emperor Avitus who had
raped his wife.[60] Similarly, Gregory's account of how Childeric (died c. 481)
was for a time replaced by Aegidius becomes in Fredegar's hands an elaborate tale, with a host of characters, including the emperor Maurice (582–602).
The drama and immediacy of this narrative were also heightened by the use
of passages of dialogue; a practice that Fredegar resorted to even in some of
his briefest interpolations. This use of direct speech to make the narration
more graphic is even more marked in the final section of the compilation, in
which more of Fredegar's own writing is to be found. Thus the Visigothic
king Sisebut's good nature is illustrated by his being made to exclaim: 'How
wretched am I that so great a shedding of human blood should occur in my
time', on hearing of his troops' slaughtering of enemy forces.[61]

Some of his tales were clearly intended to make a point, even if only with
the advantage of hindsight; though it would not be wise to assume that
Fredegar himself was necessarily their original author. Thus, for example, he
inserted into the account of Childeric's marriage to the Thuringian queen
Basina, which he took from Gregory of Tours, an account of a series of
nocturnal visions in which the character of their descendants was foretold:
the first generation would be as 'lions, unicorns and leopards', the second
like 'bears and wolves', but the third only equivalent to 'dogs and lesser
beasts.'[62] This is unlikely to have been his own invention, in that this quasi-
biblical narrative, reminiscent of the story of Nebuchadnezzar's dream, relates
to generations of kings the last of whom died in 629. It made a point rel-
evant to the early rather than the later seventh-century. It is, though, from
distinctive or anomalous-seeming elements in the selection of the contents of
his or her compilation that any hope of identifying not the name but the
purposes and intentions of Fredegar must come.

Fredegar's politics

In a recent study Ian Wood has suggested that some of the themes that he
sees as running through the work, reflected not least in Fredegar's choice of

[59] On such processes see Michael Richter, *The Formation of the Medieval West: Studies in
the Oral Culture of the Barbarians* (Dublin, 1994).

[60] Gregory of Tours, II. 9 (here following his late Roman source Sulpicius Alexander);
Fredegar III. 7, ed. Krusch, 94.

[61] Fredegar IV. 33.

[62] Fredegar III. 12.

tales, serve as a commentary on political developments in the Frankish kingdoms in the period in which he was writing.[63] He considers that Fredegar 'exposes a political world in which kings had to be ruthless, but in which ruthlessness could become tyrannical; in which queens could act as forces for good, but could equally be forces for ill; in which the aristocracy ought to cooperate, but often did not; and in which Austrasia did best when most independent.'[64] The period in which these lessons might be most pertinent would seem to be that of the establishment of the child king Childeric II (662–75) on the Austrasian throne in 662, under the regency of queen Chimnechild, the widow of Sigibert III. He therefore concludes that Fredegar's work 'is the supreme political tract of the 660s'. If so it must be admitted that it did not have many rivals, and the argument has to depend both on assumptions as to what the contents of the missing sections relating to the period 642–c. 659 might have consisted of, and on confidence that the work was written or revised around 662/3. The latter cannot be taken for granted, as the year 658/9 can only be taken as the *terminus ante quem non* for the compiling of the work, and the contents of the lost or more probably never-written final section can never be recovered. Even so, this opens up a fruitful line of approach to this work, which goes beyond the restraints of the arguments over authorship, without falling into the temptations that afflicted Schnürer and Baudot of combing the contents of the chronicle to try to identify the real Fredegar.

One element in the final section of the work that particularly drew Baudot's attention, and which still must seem one of the distinguishing features of it, are the number of references to individuals and events concerned with the *Pagus Ultrajuranus* or Transjuran region, an area not much otherwise represented in the history of the early Frankish period. While there is a marked presence of Transjuran events and persons in the narrative relating to the period c. 590–615, this falls away dramatically thereafter. The last of the Transjuran dukes to receive explicit mention by Fredegar is Herpo, who was killed in 613/4.[65] It is also quite notable that no stories relating to the *Pagus Ultrajuranus* can be found inserted into the earlier parts of the chronicle, including the epitome of Gregory of Tours. Had Fredegar been a Transjuran it is surprising that he apparently did not know of at least one individual or a single event concerned with the region in the period before 584. It is also notable that among his many minor sources there can be found no trace of

---

[63] Wood 1994b, 361–6.

[64] *ibid.* 364.

[65] Fredegar IV. 43 for Herpo, who succeeded Eudila in 613. It is possible that a *dux* Wandalmar recorded in 635 and a *dux* Wandalbert active in 642 were related to the former *Dux Ultrajuranus* Wandalmar (591–604) but this is not stated to be so by Fredegar: IV 78 and 90.

the only historical work known to have been produced in this region, the Chronicle of Bishop Marius of Avenches, which ends in 581.[66] It is particularly notable that while Fredegar records the death of Theodefrid, *Dux Ultrajuranus*, in 591, he makes no mention of his succession to the duchy in 573, an event that was reported by Marius.[67] Although Fredegar's reference to Wifflisburg as the new name for Aventicum (Avenches) has been seen as establishing a particularly close relationship between him and the town, and leading to Krusch, Schnürer and others making one or more of their 'Fredegars' a citizen of it, the lack of any trace of the one historical text produced in it, and the lack of other indications of special concern with it, must cast doubt on this line of argument.[68] While there is a marked Transjuran element in part of the final section of the chronicle, it is not consistent enough to lead us directly to its author. Once again it looks as if what is at issue is another unidentified strand in the complex web of Fredegar's sources. He had a quantity of Transjuran information, which tails off dramatically as the narrative moves closer to the period of composition. He was, therefore, not necessarily himself a native of the region.

The association of Fredegar with a particular region is, from this and other examples, an almost impossible task. For those who espoused the theories of multiple authorship apparent shifts in geographical perspective or political allegiance in the contents of the final section of the chronicle could be rationalized in terms of the differences between the three or two contributors. For adherents of single authorship these traits in the narrative require explanation in terms of the author's mobility, either physical or political. Making him a cleric, and above all a monk, somewhat inhibits this approach. Overall, Fredegar makes a number of references to places in Burgundy, including Avenches and the *Pagus Ultrajuranus*, Auxerre, Autun, Chalon-sur-Saône, and Lyon. He also records events and individuals concerned with Austrasia, with a relatively frequent mention of Metz.[69] But he can also lead his readers to Orléans, and the Loire valley, as well as to Paris and the Seine. As generations of commentators have come to realize, the range is too great to locate him in a particular geographical viewpoint. It is equally possible to mark out those parts of the Frankish kingdoms that he tells us little or nothing about. While Alamannia and the Alamans feature fairly frequently, there is only one reference to the Bavarians. Aquitaine is only mentioned once in the final section, as is the Auvergne, and so on. The problem of using such evidence

---

[66] *Marii episcopi Aventicensis Chronica*, ed. T. Mommsen, *MGH AA*, vol. XI, pp. 225–39.

[67] Marius of Avenches, ed. Mommsen, s.a. 573, preserved in a single tenth cenury manuscript from St Trond; Fredegar IV. 4 and 13. In Mommsen's correlation some of Marius's dates appear to be wrong by a factor of one year, and so 572 might be preferred.

[68] See also Frei 1969.

[69] Kusternig edition, 13: 'Seine Mannesjahre dürfte er jedoch in Metz verbracht haben ...'.

as a way of localizing Fredegar is compounded by the difficulty, or indeed the impossibility, of knowing precisely which of his reports come from earlier written sources. It is quite possible that the heavy emphasis in the period 584–613 on events in Burgundy is a reflection of the set of Burgundian annals that some scholars have seen as lying behind this section of the narrative.[70] Even were the existence of this hypothetical text to be proved, his use of it would not *per se* prove that Fredegar was working in Burgundy, as he clearly also had access to literary sources that originated outside the Frankish kingdoms entirely.

A possible indicator of his location, and more significantly of his political allegiance, may come from the system of regnal dating used for structuring the contents of the final section of his work. This would seem promising, in that for the period 584–613 the Burgundian perspective of the contents of the chronicle is reinforced by it being dated according to the regnal years of king Theuderic II of Burgundy (596–613). However, with the death of Theuderic and the elimination of his son Sigibert II (613), Fredegar then begins to date the events he describes by the regnal years of Chlotar II (584–629). These he calculates from the beginning of Chlotar's reign in Neustria in 584 rather than from his taking over of Burgundy. Thus 613 is described as being the thirtieth year of Chlotar. He continues to use the regnal years of Chlotar, even after the latter's son Dagobert was made king of Austrasia in 623. Not until Chlotar's death in 629 does Fredegar begin dating by the regnal years of Dagobert, which, however he counts from the king's installation in Austrasia. Thus, 629 is Dagobert's seventh year as well as being his father's forty-fifth. He died, according to Fredegar in the sixteenth year of his reign, and dating of the events immediately following is by the regnal years of his legitimate son Clovis II (639–57), who ruled over both Neustria and Burgundy. However, this does not prove consistent: when events in Austrasia are mentioned, these are dated by the reign of Dagobert I's other son Sigibert III (633–56). As he had been installed as king in Austrasia during his father's lifetime his regnal years are deemed to start at that point, and thus do not synchronize with those of Clovis II.

One consequence of this is that the narrative can become ragged. Events in Austrasia are recorded for the eighth and tenth years of Sigibert III only, and these are sandwiched between others relating to the third and fourth years of Clovis II. How Fredegar would have got himself out of this difficulty of structuring by regnal year but only giving the year of the king in whose kingdom the event described took place cannot be known. While there was clearly a single dominant figure, such as Chlotar II in 613–29 and Dagobert I in 629–39, it was easy for him to date everything by the years of their

---

[70] Wallace-Hadrill edition, xxii: ' … finds Burgundian annals for the period ?584–604 … '.

reigns and to ignore those of the junior partners in Austrasia, but from 639 onwards Fredegar obviously felt unable to do this. It might to us seem more sensible to have equated each calendar year with the regnal years of both kings, but it is likely that the regnal years were calculated from the actual day of royal inauguration rather than from the preceding first day of the calendar year. Thus, the relationship between the regnal years of Sigibert III and those of Clovis II would not remain constant. Politically, the only clue to be garnered from this section of the narrative is the fact that Fredegar referred to all four of the years of the reign of Clovis II in the period 639– 42, although he had not much to say about them, while only mentioning two of those of Sigibert III. It is possible that he was going to make the chronology of the reign of Clovis II, who would also outlast his half-brother by a year, the mainstay of the structure of this part of the chronicle. But, as with so much else, the abrupt ending of the work prevents any certainty.

Thwarted in the approaches to the problem of locating Fredegar through clusters of geographical references in his work or from his use of regnal chronology, some students of Fredegar have tried to identify significant emphases or particular enthusiasms that might provide a clue. Thus it has been felt there is something revealing in his apparent enthusiasm for the Arnulfing dynasty of Mayors of the palace of Austrasia, not least for Grimoald.[71] The Austrasian interest has been thought not to lie well with the author's otherwise predominantly Burgundian outlook and concerns, and Grimoald, whose career was potentially fatal to his family's political achievements and hopes, could be made to seem an unlikely subject for praise. Fredegar might, therefore, be suspected of being partial towards the Arnulfing dynasty as a whole, and in consequence more likely to have been resident in Austrasia than in Burgundy, at least in the early 660s.

Ian Wood has suggested that Fredegar's Burgundian affiliations were directed more towards the incoming Frankish ruling class in Burgundy, the *Burgundofarones* than towards the indigenous inhabitants, the *Burgundiones*.[72] As has already been indicated, the strong Burgundian element in the early part of the final section of the chronicle could reflect more the influence of particular sources than the compiler's location. It is thus not necessary to postulate a Burgundian phase followed by an Austrasian one for our author, either in terms of his geographical location or his political allegiances. He could have come from or lived in either of these two kingdoms. However, the question of Fredegar's apparently favourable verdict on Grimoald remains potentially significant, as it could be argued that anyone writing around the

---

[71] Wood 1994b, 365, ' ... the faction of Grimoald which Fredegar himself supported'.
[72] Wood 1994b, 360, with references.

year 660 could only contemplate giving such an impression if they lived in
the Austrasian kingdom.

Having, after a brief struggle, succeeded his father Pippin I as Mayor of
the Palace in Austrasia around 643, Grimoald probably remained the dominant
figure at the court of the Austrasian king Sigibert III (633–56) until the latter's death in 656.[73] In a very surprising manoeuvre, reported in the *Liber
Historiae Francorum*, and also alluded to in Stephanus's early eighth-century
Vita of Bishop Wilfrid of York, on Sigibert's death, his only son and heir the
child Dagobert (II) was sent off into exile in Ireland, while Grimoald installed
a son of his own called Childebert on the throne.[74] He himself did not long
survive this coup, as in some unexplained fashion he fell into the hands of the
Neustrian Frankish king Clovis II, who had him executed. As Clovis II (639–
57) died in 657, this must have occurred either in that year or late in 656. As
for Childebert, he was able to retain the Austrasian throne relatively untrou-
bled until his own death, from unknown causes, probably in 662.

Burgundy formed part of the Neustrian kingdom of Clovis II and his heirs,
and if Fredegar was a partisan of Grimoald then a location for our author in
Austrasia, at least in the period 657/62, must be thought to be highly probable. However, the Arnulfing and Austrasian connections of Fredegar can be
exaggerated. Of Grimoald he has effectively three things to say. Firstly,
Fredegar states that like his father he was popular. Secondly he records that
there was a struggle between him and a certain Otto, who had held the rank
of *Baiolus* in the court of Sigibert III, over the succession to the office of
Mayor when Grimoald's father Pippin I died in 640/1. This was resolved by
the murder of Otto in 643, carried out by Lantfrid duke of the Alamanni at
Grimoald's instigation. Thirdly, he and a duke Adalgisel took particularly care
to protect the young king Sigibert III in the course of his disastrous battle
against the rebel Thuringian duke Radulf.[75] All of this hardly amounts to a
eulogy; nor can it be known what would have been said of him in later sections of the work. Fredegar was not necessarily consistent in his verdicts, as
can be seen in his account of Dagobert I (623–39); but it would be fairer to
say that he did not expect that those whom he praised on one occasion could
not be blamed on another.[76]

---

[73] Ewig 1993, 143–6, 181–5.

[74] *Liber Historiae Francorum* ch. 43; *Vita Wilfridi* ch. 28, ed. B. Colgrave, *The Life of Bishop
Wilfrid by Eddius Stephanus* (Cambridge, 1927), 54; for some differing interpretations of the
chronology and significance of these events see Gerberding 1987, 47–66, and Picard 1991.
Becher 1994 doubts the credibility of the *LHF* here, and suggests that Childebert was a true
Merovingian, posibly an illegitimate son of Sigibert III, who was adopted by Grimoald after
his father's death. If ultimately unprovable, this seems a more probable explanation.

[75] Fredegar IV. 86–8.

[76] Or that those whose virtues he extolled could not be criticized for their weaknesses: as
for example, Aega (IV. 80), who is both extensively eulogized but also blamed for 'avarice'.

From what he wrote about Grimoald, Fredegar cannot necessarily be described as being a supporter of the Arnulfings. To say that in 640/1 Grimoald was popular 'with many' in Austrasia need be no more than the truth, and his involvement in the murder of Otto is neither concealed nor justified. Fredegar was, however, unambiguously enthusiastic about Grimoald's father Pippin I, and the latter's brother-in-law bishop Arnulf of Metz. The latter is referred to by Fredegar as *beatissimus*: 'most blessed', and he is ascribed with the quality of *sanctitas*.[77] This could be contrasted with the treatment of Pippin I's ally, bishop Chunibert of Cologne, who, although a significant figure in Austrasian politics in the period c. 630–40, is never qualified by any epithet whatsoever. Arnulf's sanctity makes him a mediator in the quarrels between Chlotar II (584–629) and his son Dagobert I (623–39). His advice and that of Pippin I are said to contribute directly to the prosperity and renown of Dagobert's rule. After his retirement (to a life of ascetic seclusion) around the year 629, his brother-in-law Pippin is presented as the mainstay of Dagobert's regime in Austrasia: 'more cautious than others, a true counsellor, most loyal and respected by all for his love of justice'.[78]

Although the two founding figures of this important dynasty, that made itself the new royal house of Francia in 751, receive unstinting praise from Fredegar, he does not give his favours in a partisan way. Bishop Austrenus of Orléans (587–post 604) is also called *beatissimus*, although we are told no more about him.[79] Even more strikingly, Pippin's contemporary, the Neustrian Mayor of the Palace Aega (d. 641/2) receives equal measure of praise from Fredegar. He is described as being 'amongst other Neustrians the most assiduous in his advice to Dagobert I', and was entrusted with responsibility for queen Nantechildis and the infant Clovis (II) by the dying king out of respect for his valuable counsel.[80] He held the office of Mayor in Neustria during the first three years of Clovis II's reign, and Fredegar's verdict on him was highly favourable: 'Aega was truly outstanding amongst the other leading men of Neustria, acting with prudence and imbued with the fullness of patience. He was noble by birth, very wealthy, a follower of justice, erudite in his speech and always ready with advice.'[81] His successor as Mayor of the Palace in Neustria, Erchinoald, was also highly esteemed by Fredegar, who called him 'patient', 'full of goodness', 'humble', and 'benevo-

---

[77] Fredegar IV. 52, 53, and 58; the martyr bishop Desiderius of Vienne is called *sanctus*: IV. 32.

[78] Fredegar IV 53, 58 and 61.

[79] Fredegar IV. 25; the only other thing certainly known of him is the date of his succession to the see of Orléans, given in Gregory of Tours, *Historiae*, IX. 18, ed. Krusch, *MGH SRM* 1, 432.

[80] Fredegar IV. 62 and 79.

[81] Fredegar IV. 80.

lent' towards the bishops and all other men, and lacking in pride or greed. He was 'loved by all'.[82]

As these examples show, Fredegar was in no sense an exclusive partisan of the Arnulfings or of Austrasia over Neustria. His verdict on Erchinoald was given in the past tense and was thus written after the latter's death, which has to be placed between 657 and 659.[83] This is a further indicator to the fact that this section of the chronicle was being written around or after 659. It is also notable that it was delivered on the man who as Neustrian Mayor, must have been involved with Clovis II in the capture and killing of Grimoald in 656/7. If Fredegar had been an Arnulfing and Austrasian apologist, writing under the rule of Grimoald's son, as he has sometimes been presented, it would be hard to comprehend why he gave so favourable a report of this Neustrian Mayor of the Palace. The probable implication is that he was writing in the kingdom of Neustria and Burgundy, rather than in Austrasia.[84]

What is clear from the kind of judgements that Fredegar makes on the great men of the 630s and early 640s, not excluding king Dagobert I, is that he looked for particular virtues. Devotion to justice is marked out as a special quality in Pippin I, Aega and king Dagobert, at least before he fell into evil ways. Prudence and the giving of good advice are other characteristics for which all of these men are highly commended. Dagobert is criticized both for debauchery after he took over the Neustrian kingdom in 629 and for cupidity towards the properties of the Church and the magnates.[85] Dagobert is also blamed for cutting back on his generosity towards the Church, but it is noteworthy that the virtues that Fredegar specifically praises do not include almsgiving and the making of ecclesiastical endowments. These aspects of his thinking might again give support to the suggestion that he was a pious layman rather than a cleric or a monk.

Fredegar's strongly expressed approval for many of the leading men in both kingdoms in the late 630s and early 640s is very personal. He does not give the impression that he is merely passing on other people's views. The opinions he gives have the character of ones formed at first hand. Thus, if Fredegar had direct experience of the royal courts it was likely to have occurred or to have commenced in this period. The breadth of his knowledge, not least his access to information coming from beyond the frontiers of

---

[82] Fredegar IV. 84.

[83] Gerberding 1987, 67 and n.1.

[84] Wood 1994a, 230–8 for the politics of this period. On the other hand, Fredegar could have been writing some years after the early 660s; at a time when the Arnulfings had returned to power in Austrasia and when there were no formal grounds for hostility between that kingdom and Neustria-Burgundy, but the earliest point at which such conditions could be said to occur would be 679/80.

[85] Fredegar IV. 60, where his thoughts are said to have turned away from God.

Francia, may also result from connections with the highest levels of Frankish society. His knowledge of Columbanian monasticism is less surprising when it be appreciated how much noble patronage of monastic houses took place in the mid-seventh-century, not least by Erchinoald and by the Arnulfings. Whether Fredegar was a layman or a cleric is hard, even impossible, finally to determine. His presentation of royal and aristocratic virtues is by no means ecclesiastical in character, and there is no reason why as a pious layman he should not have thought it reprehensible of Dagobert I to cut back on his gifts to the Church. There are no references to the miraculous in his work, and it is clear that in his version of the epitome of the first six books of Gregory of Tours, the selection favours royal and secular events rather than ecclesiastical ones. Other elements in his narrative, such as the reference to Erchinoald's humility towards the bishops could be cited to give an opposite effect. Overall, while the balance of probability might be thought to favour the view that Fredegar was a layman of high status, writing in the Neustrian-Burgundian kingdom around the year 660, the evidence is not strong enough to command complete conviction.

Fredegar's language

Fredegar's orthography and grammar, which are taken to be more or less identical to those of Lucerius the scribe of the earliest manuscript, have attracted almost as much attention and certainly more derision than his skills as a historian.[86] While his text has sometimes been taken as a hunting ground for the earliest signs of Romance, most commentators have addressed the topic from the standpoint of his falling away from the standards of pure or classical Latin, either from the Roman past or as would be revived in the succeeding Carolingian period. The verdict, as magisterially delivered by Wallace-Hadrill in the opening sentence of his section on Fredegar's language, is one of condemnation: 'The language of Fredegar is not a language with a future; it is far removed from the Classical Latin from which it derived, far removed also from Romance, the parent of modern French.'[87] However, he goes on to point out that the only fair point of comparison is that of other seventh-century Frankish Latin texts, and draws attention to its similarity to contemporary legal formulae and inscriptions.[88] Even so, he continues to describe

---

[86] Haag 1899 is the most substantial by far, and most prone to take a starting point in classical norms.

[87] Wallace-Hadrill edition, xxviii; for this section of the introduction to his edition, which takes up nearly a third of the whole, he was advised by the Romance scholar Frank J. Barnet. See also the linguistic section of the introduction to Kusternig's edition, 18–33, which is more analytical and less judgemental.

[88] Goffart 1961, 692, adds the fact of resemblances to the language of seventh-century Merovingian charters, citing Book Four chapter 55 as a particularly good point of comparison.

it as 'barbaric'.[89] While quite a lot of the detailed content of the analysis of 'Phonology' and of 'Morphology and Syntax' offered in the Wallace-Hadrill edition would continue to be accepted by linguists, the wider cultural context and the expectations about the nature, function, and influences on the written language in this period would now seem dated.[90] A new study of Fredegar's language is needed.[91]

The Continuators

The manuscript evidence, and the limited use of the work by others, including the anonymous author of the *Liber Historiae Francorum* of 726/7, indicates that Fredegar's probably unfinished text did not circulate widely in the course of the decades following his death. In the eighth-century, however, it was given a new lease of life by the addition of a number of continuations to its account of recent events. While the importance of these sections of new material, especially relating to the period from 721 to 768, has long been recognized, or even taken for granted, the questions of the number, dating and purposes of these continuations has never aroused the amount of interest or of controversy that was generated by the arguments over the original Fredegar compilation.[92] Thus, while the bibliography relating to the authorial and structural problems of the latter is substantial, hardly anything has been written about the Continuations, widely though they have been used as evidence for eighth-century Frankish history. A generally accepted view of this text as the 'family chronicle' of the Arnulfing house has also tended to overvalue its authority and obscure its real compositional purposes.[93]

The chronology and construction of the Continuations were first seriously considered by Krusch; his conclusions were incorporated into the authoritative Wattenbach-Levison manual on Frankish historical sources and have been

---

[89] Roger Wright (personal communication) has commented that such a term could only be acceptable if meaning 'used by Germanic speakers', rather than, as seems to be implied here, 'hopelessly corrupt'. This observation also raises an interesting question about Fredegar's own linguistic and ethnic background, which requires further consideration.

[90] This would not involve conceeding that Fredegar was anything approaching a good literary stylist: Michel Banniard, *Genèse culturelle de l'Europe (Ve–VIIIe siècle)* (Paris, 1989), 102.

[91] For some signposts to the basis on which such a study would be undertaken see Roger Wright (ed.), *Latin and the Romance Languages in the Early Middle Ages* (London, 1991), and Michel Banniard, *Viva Voce: communication écrite et communication orale du IVeau IXesiècle en Occident latin* (Paris, 1992).

[92] For example, Teodor Breysig, *Jahrbücher des fränkischen Reichs, 714–41* (Leipzig, 1869).

[93] Gustav Schnürer, *Kirche und Kultur im Mittelalter* (2nd edn Paderborn, 1927) vol.1, 251, and Wallace-Hadrill edition, xxvi.

accepted almost entirely by the modern editors of the work.[94] According to Krusch, the text of the Continuations, to be found primarily in the fourth class of manuscripts, can be divided into a number of discrete sections, nearly all of which represent a further stage in the process of continuing the original work, mostly by different individuals at different times. Following the chapter divisions of the modern editions, these sections equate to chapters 1–10, 11–17, 18–21, 22–33, and 34–54.

The text of the first of these is an almost exact copy of what Krusch categorized as the 'B' or Austrasian recension of the anonymous *Liber Historiae Francorum*, first composed at St Denis or Soissons around 726/7.[95] This, it is argued, was taken as a useful bridging text to cover the period between the abrupt termination of the original Fredegar compilation with the events of 642 and the late 720s. To this ready-made section, which he slightly augmented, the first continuator added some new material of his own (chapters 11–17), bringing the narrative up to 735. The second Continuation has been seen as being the work of two distinct authors, possibly writing at slightly different times. The first, adding only chapters 18 to 21, took the account up to 739, while the second went on from that point to the consecration of Pippin as king of the Franks in 751. A final continuation, the longest section of all, subsequently advanced the narrative through the reign of Pippin, ending with the royal consecration of his sons Charles and Carloman in 768.

That a break existed in the text between what was written c. 751 and the final section concluding in 768 is proved by the survival in one manuscript, Vatican MS Reginensis lat. 213, of a colophon, which has been translated as follows: 'Up to this point, the illustrious Count Childebrand, uncle of the said King Pippin, took great pains to have his history or "geste" of the Franks recorded. What follows is by authority of the illustrious Count Nibelung, Childebrand's son.'[96] Thus, the final section of the Continuations, covering 751–68, was commissioned by Count Nibelung; what went before was written for his father.

Both Childebrand and Nibelung are shadowy figures in the records of eighth-century Francia, despite their closeness to the new royal house. The nature of Childebrand's link to the Carolingian dynasty has been debated. It

---

[94] Krusch 1882, 495–515, *idem*, edition, 8-9; Wattenbach-Levison, II, 161–3; Wallace-Hadrill edition xxv–xxviii, xliii–xlv; Kusternig edition, 7–9. Ganshof 1970(b), 24–5, believed in only three continuators, whose work corresponded to chs 1–17, 18–33 and 34–54 respectively.

[95] Gerberding 1987 argues from the existence of a hybrid text in MS Paris BN lat. 7906 that the independent existence of this second recension cannot be proved for a date earlier than the 790s, but the palaeographic evidence for the priority of this manuscript is far from certain, nor is this the only conclusion to which it might lead.

[96] Translation from Wallace-Hadrill edition, 102–3.

was once generally thought that he must have been a half-brother of Charles Martel, the son of the latter's mother Alpaida by some other liaison. In 1946 Léon Levillain, who had previously been the leading proponent of this theory, demonstrated that the word used here for 'uncle', *avunculus*, could not have been applied to his relationship to Pippin if this had been the case. Instead, he argued, Childebrand had to be a son of Pippin II by a concubine.[97]

Although this textual division is clear, even if only testified to in one manuscript, the others detected by Krusch and endorsed by succeeding editors are less so.[98] Class 4 manuscripts contain all of the text of the Continuations or none of it. Thus, no manuscripts survive containing variant forms of the text of the Continuations or offering only some of the supposed sections. The stylistic arguments in favour of multiple authorship of the Continuations are of the same kind as those first used in the 1880s to buttress the arguments in favour of multiple authorship of the original Fredegar compilation, and which are now largely discredited. Arguments relating to particular features of the contents of the Continuations which might indicate compositional breaks, such as the chronological calculations that make up chapter 17, are also liable to reinterpretation. These calculations, dating to 735, could have been incorporated into the Continuations directly from another manuscript that the compiler was using. It was in this way that calculations referring to the year 613 came to appear in the original Fredegar collection, leading Krusch to argue, ultimately unconvincingly, that the year 613 must have played an important role in the compositional history of the work.

The belief in multiple authorship of the Continuations has also taken no cognisance of the fact that the addition of sections of new material to the mid seventh-century Fredegar compilation is not the only change that was made to it. The work of Fredegar was given a major revision: the five-book structure imposed in or soon after Fredegar's own day, and attested to by the manuscripts of the first three classes, gave way to a new three-book structure. In this the *Liber Generationis* and the papal and imperial lists were dropped entirely and replaced by the *De Cursu Temporum* of Quintus Julius Hilarian. This was incorporated with Fredegar's epitome of the chronicles of Jerome and Hydatius to constitute a new Book One. Furthermore, an idosyncratic text of the pseudonymous *Fall of Troy* of 'Dares the Phrygian' was inserted into the text of Jerome, between chapters three and four, to augment the information relating to the theme of the Trojan origin of the

---

[97] Levillain 1946, 30.

[98] Although the colophon itself is absent, there is a clear break in the text, distinguished by a two-line space and the use of decorated initial, at the same point in MS London, British Library, Harley 3771 and similarly in MS Milan Archivo Capitolare di Sant' Ambrogio M.13. Significantly, this is the only such division in the text of the Continuations in these MSS.

Franks. Fredegar's version of the epitome of the first six books of Gregory of Tours became Book Two of the new edition, and the third book was made up of Fredegar's own contributions, the former Book Five, to which the Continuations were added without a break. There are also a number of textual alterations to be found throughout the work, which have to be associated with this revision. All in all, the Fredegar compilation had been streamlined, to make it more clearly a history of the Franks, within an overarching structure extending from Creation up to the reviser's lifetime. This may make it more likely that the colophon in MS Vatican Reginensis 213 gives a clue to the intention and even the title of the work in its new form – *Historia vel gesta Francorum*. That the only provable break in the text of the Continuations occurs following the consecration of Pippin in 751 may support the suggestion that this *Historia Francorum*, in the form of a thorough revision and extension of Fredegar's seventh-century work, was undertaken at that time to mark the inauguration of the new *Rex Francorum*.[99] That it was commissioned by Childebrand, the new king's uncle, could indicate that Pippin was the intended dedicatee. The continuation of this revised Fredegar in 768, following the consecration of Pippin's sons, may thus hardly be accidental. The work compiled to honour the first Carolingian was thus brought up to date as a gift for his successors. It would seem possible to think of the revised Fredegar compilation of 751 as Childebrand's *Historia Francorum* and that of 768 as Nibelung's recension of the work. In neither case, however, was the task carried out by them in person. A monastic scriptorium under their patronage would be a likely venue for the carrying out of such a task, but no indications exist that might give its location, other than for the probability that it was in Burgundy.[100]

Such a genesis could have important implications for the authority of some of the contents of the Continuations, as, if only for convenience, this eighth-century section will continue to be called. If the narrative, especially relating to the 730s, was not put together by one or two contemporary authors, but rather by a single compiler working around the year 751 then the degree of confidence that can be placed in it may have to be modified. Certainly, closer inspection of the text suggests that it is rather less obviously a piece of contemporary reporting than has often been assumed. Comparison with some of the sets of eighth-century Minor Annals can be particularly revealing.[101] Campaigns by Charles Martel that these report for the years 720, 721,

---

[99] Collins 1994(a), 235–46.

[100] Levillain 1937, 343–46, and Wallace-Hadrill edition, xxvi–xxvii, for the location of the few known estates of this family.

[101] Texts in Georg Pertz (ed.) *MGH SS* 1, 6–10 and 22–5; on these see Wattenbach-Levison. II, 180–92.

722, 725, and 729 find no mention in the Continuations. Instead, there is a three- or four-year gap in the latter's narrative corresponding to the period 721–4. Three events that can otherwise be dated to the period 724–8 are then reported but given no chronology, and there follows another gap in the narrative, from 728 to 731, in which nothing is recorded. For the early 730s, while the quantity of material included increases, the quality of its organization if anything deteriorates. The Aquitanian war of 731 is said to be contemporaneous with the Bavarian campaign of 728. The Aquitanian expedition of 731 is also made to be identical with the Poitiers campaign of 732 or 733. Finally, a section relating to military activity in Frisia is located quite outside its actual chronological context. As the achievement of an author supposedly writing in 735 this lack of content, factual error and chronological imprecision is hard to credit. His putative successor of 739 is little better, for in the small section credited to him he conflates campaigns fought in Provence in 737 and 739 into a single episode.[102]

For the events in Francia following the death of Charles Martel in 741 and preceding the consecration of Pippin in 751, the Continuations are by any argument a major source, and a relatively substantial one too. Although this period was later to be covered again in the earliest section of the *Annales Regni Francorum*, this account largely derived from the Continuations, though in much abbreviated form. On the other hand, the origin of this revised Fredegar compilation in the patronage of Pippin's uncle Childebrand gave it an obvious political bias. The military achievements of Pippin and Carloman are given a triumphal gloss that hardly corresponds with the realities of what is described. That the two Mayors appointed a new Merovingian king in the person of Childeric III (743–51) is never mentioned. On retiring into monastic life in 747, Carloman is said to have handed over his kingdom and his son to Pippin; statements that can be demonstrated to be untrue.[103] The survival and continued opposition to Pippin up until 753 of Carloman's son Drogo is just one feature of the resistance to the first king of the Carolingian dynasty that this source obscures or omits.[104]

Although it provided a substantial and partisan narrative of the events of his father's reign, the revised Fredegar seems to have fallen out of favour in the time of Charlemagne (768–814). Rather than adding any further continuations to the Fredegar corpus, the probably palatine *Annales Regni Francorum* started a new historiographical compilation. The limited use and deliberate compression in that work of the Fredegar entries relating to the reign of

---

[102] Collins 1994(a), 245–6.

[103] Becher 1989.

[104] Michael J. Enright, *Iona, Tara, Soissons* (Berlin and New York, 1985), 108–19 for some of Pippin's problems; see also Horst Ebling, 'Die inneraustrasische Opposition' in Jarnut, Nonn and Richter (1994), 295–304.

Pippin was partly prompted by certain embarrassing features to be found in them. In particular, the statement of the Fredegar Continuator that Pippin had divided Aquitaine equally between Charlemagne and his brother Carloman (768–71) contradicted all of the historiography of the former's reign, which consistently made him out to be the chosen recipient of this region. In 769 Charlemagne and Carloman seem to have fallen out over their respective claims to Aquitaine. It is possible, too, that the final version of the Fredegar compilation, prepared for the royal coronations of 768, was presented primarily or exclusively to Carloman, as Count Nibelung's main landed interests may have lain in his kingdom rather than Charlemagne's.[105] Whatever the truth of this speculation, it is clear that the career of the Fredegar compilation as a self-contained and expandable corpus of historical texts finally came to an end in this period. Some of the information it contained, particularly in the Continuations, was still regarded as useful, and could be excerpted for inclusion in such newer compilations as the *Annales Mettenses Priores*, written probably in the convent of Chelles around 805/6, and the *Chronicle of Moissac*, which was put together in south-western Francia about 818.[106] But no attempt was made to augment Fredegar's own work or that of the Continuators. When it was revived in the ninth-century, with the Class 5 manuscripts, it was seen only as an appendix to a newly enhanced text of Gregory of Tours, and no longer as an independent historiographical compilation in its own right. Only that section of the text mostly unavailable in other forms, that is, covering the period 584–741, was included as a 'Book Ten' of his *Historiae* in the manuscripts of this class, which might better be thought of as a class of the manuscripts of Gregory rather than one of those of Fredegar. Evidence of use of Fredegar by post-Carolingian chroniclers is slight; one major exception being Sigebert of Gembloux (d. 1112), whose chronicle indicates that he had read a manuscript of Class 4.[107]

---

[105] See note 91 above.

[106] *Annales Mettenses Priores*, ed. B. de Simson, *MGH SRG* (Hanover, 1905); see Nelson 1991, 156-60; also Irene Haselbach, *Aufsteig und Herrschaft der Karlinger in der Darstellung der Annales Mettenses Priores* (Lübeck and Hamburg, 1970), who favours St Denis as the place of composition. There is probable evidence of the use of Fredegar in the ninth-century second version of the *Passio Leudegarii*, written in Poitiers; see the notes to Krusch, *MGH SRM* V, 333–5 and Fouracre 1990, 13–21. The *Chronicle of Moissac* is in *MGH SS* I, 280–313, and uses material from a Class 4 manuscript of Fredegar, including the Continuations.

[107] *PL* 160, cc. 112–46: the earliest indication relates to events of 594; the latest to those of 768.

BIBLIOGRAPHY

Manuscripts

The manuscript tradition of the *Chronicle of Fredegar* was first given a substantial scholarly study in an article of almost two hundred pages that Bruno Krusch published in *Neues Archiv* in 1882, to accompany and justify his edition. A briefer account of the manuscripts will be found in that edition, and also in the two subsequent ones published by Michael Wallace-Hadrill in 1960 and by Andreas Kusternig in 1982. Essentially the latter two followed most aspects of Krusch's reconstruction except where the publication of Hellmann's study in 1934 had showed that one major modification was required. The individual manuscripts themselves had of course been studied and commented upon by a variety of palaeographers since Krusch's time, but, rightly or wrongly, none of these contributions led to any other modification of his *stemma codicum*.

Class 1
1.   Paris, Bibliothèque Nationale, MS fonds lat. 10910 (*c.* 679 or c. 714/5?).**1**
2.   Metz, Bibliothèque Municipale, MS 134 (*c.* 768–91), destroyed 1944. **1ˣ**

Class 2
3.   Bern, Burgerbibliothek, MS 318 (mid C9). **2ᵃ**
4.   London, British Library, MS Harley 5251 (C9). **2ᵇ**

Class 3
5.   Leiden, Bibliotek des Rijksuniversiteit, MS Vossianus Q. 5 (*c.* 800). **3¹**
6.   Rome, Vatican Library, MS Reginenses latini 713 (*c.* 800). **3²**
7.   Vienna, Österreichische Nationalbibliothek, MS 482 (late C8/early C9). **3ᵃ**
8.   Augsburg, Archiv des Bistums (formerly Bischöfliche Ordinariatsbibliothek), MS K 223, ff. 1–97v (late C15). **3ᵇ**

Class 4
9.   Rome, Vatican Library, MS Reginensis latina 213 (C9/10). **4ᵇ**
10.   Troyes, Bibliothèque Municipale, MS 802, ff. 104r–115r (first half C9). **4ᵃˣ**
11.   Milan, Basilica di San Ambrogio, Archivo Capitolare, MS M. 13 (last quarter C9). **4ᵇ¹**
12.   London, British Library, MS Harley 3771 (mid C9). **4ᵇ²**
13.   Munich, Bayerische Staatsbibliothek, MS clm. 4352 (C15). **4ᵇ²ˣ**

14. Montpellier, Ecole de Médécine, MS 158 (C10). **4^{c1}**
15. Paris, Bibliothèque Nationale, MS lat. 4883A (C11). **4^{c2}**
16. Leiden, Rijksuniversiteit, MS Voss. Q. 20, ff. 1–8v (C10). **4^{c3}**

Class 5

17. Heidelberg, Universitätsbibliothek, MS Palat. lat. 864, ff. 110v–134v (C8/9). **5^a**
18. Paris, Bibliothèque Nationale, MS lat. 5921 (C11). **5^{ax}**
19. Berlin, Deutsche Staatsbibliothek, MS lat. quart. 266 (C10). **5^{xa}**
20. Paris, Bibliothèque Nationale, MS lat. 9765, ff. 100r–110v (c9/10). **5^b**
21. Saint-Omer, Bibliothèque Municipale, MS 706, ff. 116v–144v (c10/11), MS. divided, now also Saint-Omer, Bibliothèque Municipale, MS 697. **5^c**
22. Brussels, Bibliothèque Royale, MS 6439–51 (C11). **5^{cx}**
23. Namur, Bibliothèque Publique, fonds de la ville 11 (C9). **5^d**
24. Brussels, Bibliothèque Royale, MS 9361–67 (C12). **5^e**
25. Vienna, Österreichische Nationalbibliothek, MS 473 (late C9). **5^f**

1 The earliest extant manuscript, Paris Bibliothèque Nationale fonds latins 10910, is written in uncial script, though probably copying a lost cursive exemplar (Fredegar's autograph?).[108] It consists of 187 folios of 235 by 168 mm written in single columns in from 16 to 24 lines per folio. It contains only the Fredegar compilation, and a version of the Chronicle of Isidore of Seville that almost certainly does not form an integral part of the latter.[109] There are line drawings on folios A (the first folio of the book), 23v and 75v. The figures in the drawings remain effectively unidentified; that on f. 75v, for example, having been described as Christ in Majesty or alternatively as being St Helena! There are also almost illegible marginal notes in contemporary Merovingian cursive on ff. 20, 58v, 69, 83, 86v, and 184v.[110]

---

[108] Its uncial is not sufficiently distinctive to feature in the attempt to characterize regional distinctions in eighth-century Frankish versions of this script: see Rosamond McKitterick, 'Frankish uncial: a new context for the work of the Echternach scriptorium', in A. Weiler and P. Bange (eds), *Willibrod zijn wereld en zijn werk* (Nijmegen, 1990), 374–88; reprinted in *eadem, Books, Scribes and Learning* as item V.

[109] This is MS 'X' of Theodor Mommsen's edition of the *Chronicle* of Isidore: *MGH AA* vol. 11, 398.

[110] *CLA* vol. V, no. 608; for examples of the text see also Delisle 1881, vol. III, plate XIII, Zimmermann 1916, vol. II plate 74 and *New Palaeographical Society* no. 181; for the illustrations Zimmermann vol. I pp. 178–9 and vol. II plate 73; Jean Hubert, Jean Porcher and W.F. Volbach, *Art of the Dark Ages* (Eng. tr. London, 1969),186–8, and Lasko 1971, plate 105 and p. 105; Lindsay 1915, 474 errs in ascribing its provenance to Clermont cathedral, and thus deceives Lesne 1938, 33; actually it once belonged to Jacques Sirmond, who donated it to the Collège de Clermont in Paris, whence it passed to the BN. On the MS see Krusch 1882, 250–8; Wallace-Hadrill1957/8, 71–2; *idem*, edition, xlvii–l; McKitterick 1981, 192 and 205 n.89, and *eadem* 1994, 99–100. David Ganz, who kindly examined this MS for me, suggests that the cursive marginalia on ff. 77v and 56r, as well as those illustrated by Delisle, are by the scribe Lucerius, who was also responsible for the initials, 'especially the fish on ff. 30v and 60r'. The Tironian notes, hitherto undeciphered, he ascribes to two different scribes. The first of these

This manuscript was written nearly a century before any of the others now extant, and would seem to be relatively close in time to the original compilation of the work, at least if the arguments for single authorship be accepted. It has to be dated primarily from a damaged colophon on its final folio. Although Krusch's reconstruction of this is not fully convincing, it can be agreed that the text implies that the scribe of the manuscript was a priest and monk called Lucerius, who was writing in the fourth year of a king Dagobert.[111] There were three Frankish kings of the name of Dagobert. The first of these reigned from 623 to 639, and thus died before the completion of the work. Although Merovingian regnal chronology of the second half of the seventh-century is by no means fully established, a second Dagobert would seem to have begun his reign between April and July 676 and to have been murdered in late December 679. This, unfortunately for present purposes, gave him part of a fourth regnal year, extending from April/July to December 679. The third Dagobert (711–15) managed a whole fourth year between January/February 714 and January/February 715, before expiring of apparently natural causes later in 715.[112] In consequence of this regrettable ambiguity, some commentators have opted for a date of 679 (though sometimes mistakenly given as 678 or even as 676/7), and others for 714/5.

One differentiating factor would be the more limited extent of Dagobert II's authority. He was king only over Austrasia, whereas Dagobert III reigned over if not ruled all of the components of Francia. Unfortunately, MS Paris 10910 is palaeographically unique. Its script has no clear and close affinities to those of other manuscripts, and it has been recognized that the statement in the authoritative *Codices Latini Antiquiores* attributing it to a Burgundian scriptorium was made on grounds of historical probability more than on palaeographical or codicological ones.[113] The nearest possible relative – 'and that not a close one' – has been seen in a mid eighth-century manuscript from Lyon.[114] Rosamond McKitterick accepts that there is some influence from Luxeuil in the script, but suspects the manuscript was 'produced in the Rhône Valley or a region near Lyon'.[115] These views must strengthen without ultimately proving a Burgundian origin, and therefore a dating to 714 and the reign of Dagobert III, but no hard and fast ruling can be made.[116] The three line drawings in the text have also proved impossible to tie closely and uncontentiously to

supplies notes to identify biblical characters who appear in the epitome of the Eusebius-Jerome chronicle. The second, writing on ff. 63v, 79r and 132r, notes Theodosius, Justinian and Antonina and Brunechildis respectively. David Ganz also offers the suggestion that the enthroned figure illustrated on f. 75v could, from its textual context, be a depiction of Clovis as Christian king.

[111] Krusch 1882, 254, and *idem*, edition, 9–10; Wallace-Hadrill edition, xlvii.

[112] For the chronology of Dagobert II see Tardif 1899, 33–58 and Levillain 1913, 78–86; for Dagobert III see Krusch, *MGH SRM* VII, 501–2.

[113] *CLA* vol. V, no. 608; Wallace-Hadrill edition, xlvii, quoting Bernhard Bischoff.

[114] David Ganz in a letter; the MS is Lyon Bibl. munic. 602 (*CLA* vol. VI, nos. 782 a/b). Some affinities with the script of the Gundohinus Gospels (*CLA* vol. VI, no. 716) may also be noticed.

[115] McKitterick 1981, 192 and 205 n.89.

[116] Goffart 1961, 694, is hostile to the Burgundian attribution of this manuscript, as all other Fredegar codices of Carolingian date are of Austrasian origin. He offers no palaeographical arguments.

other extant examples of comparable late Merovingian illumination. The earliest com-
mentator, E.H. Zimmermann in 1916 linked it to Luxeuil. More recent attempts to
link its art to that of the Gundohinus Gospels have been rejected.[117]

Where, however, a greater degree of assurance is now possible is in respect of this
manuscript's relationship to its fellows. For Krusch it was the earliest extant exemplar, from which all subsequent manuscripts descended. Hellmann showed that a
number of distinctive errors and scribal misunderstandings on the part of Lucerius
mean that none of them were copied directly from this manuscript, but instead de-
scend from a close relative of it. Thus, although both early in date and close to the
author in time, MS Paris 10910 represents a codicological cul de sac.

Whatever its faults, it provides proof that the structuring of the Fredegar corpus
by books subdivided into chapters was not an inherent part of the authorial strategy.
The chapter divisions cut across or ignore chronological divisions in the section of
new material relating to the period 584–642 and make nonsense of the author's own
structuring of the work at this point, which is by regnal years. In MS 10910 these
chapter divisions have been added by another, probably later, hand.

1ˣ The second manuscript in Class 1 was, regrettably, destroyed in 1944. It only
contained extracts from Fredegar: the *Supputatio* and lists from Book One and chapters 3-37 of Book Two. Previously it was Metz, Bibliothèque Municipale ms 134. It
consisted of 222 folios of 285 by 185 mm written in 26 single column lines per
folio (other than for a glossary on ff. 186v to 201v).[118] Bernhard Bischoff has concluded that this manuscript was written at Metz in the time of Archbishop Angilram
(768-91).[119] It was certainly in the library of St Arnulf's Metz by the tenth/eleventh-
century.

2ᵃ and 2ᵇ The two manuscripts of the second class, Bern Burgerbibliothek MS 318
and London, British Library MS Harley 5251, are also incomplete, in that they end in
the middle of what modern editions call chapter 9 of Book Four, containing the legendary tale of the conversion of the Persian Shah's wife. They are both dated to the ninth-
century.[120] Since Krusch's edition, it has been accepted that the two manuscripts are
copies from a single lost exemplar. However, there exists one significant difference
between them. Both manuscripts appear to end at an identical, grammatically nonsen-
sical, point in the chapter, and it is clear from the Bern manuscript that it contained
no more of the work. However, the lower part of the verso of the final folio of the
Harley manuscript has been erased, but there are visible indications that the text continued on for at least two more lines, if not more. The bizarre termination in mid-
sentence that is due to erasure in the Harley manuscript, but quite inexplicable in the

---

[117] Zimmermann 1916 vol. I, 178–9; Lasko 1971, 105; Nees 1987, 2 and n.4.

[118] *CLA* vol. VI, no. 788; see Krusch 1882, 258–65; Wallace-Hadrill edition, l; for an example of its script see Krusch edition, facing p. 10; on its illustration see Holter 1965, 77.

[119] Bischoff 1994, 23; Lowe in *CLA* VI, no. 788 sees it as being 'written in a centre apparently under the influence of the school which produced the Ada-group codices'.

[120] Wallace-Hadrill edition l, giving Bischoff's opinion that Harley MS 5251 is 'late 9th-
century, French'.

Bern codex might suggest that the latter is a copy of the former. Both manuscripts concur in a faulty numeration of the chapters of the final book, caused by labelling the Prologue as chapter 1. In consequence the ninth chapter is numbered the tenth.

2ª Bern, Burgerbibliothek 318, consists of 131 folios of 255 by 180 mm (175 × 120) in 17 gatherings, written in single columns of 23 lines. Five folios are missing and f. 131 is blank. The Caroline minuscule employed for the script has been assigned to the mid-ninth-century and to western Francia.[121] On folio 130r an inscription identifies the scribe as an otherwise unknown Hecpert. The Fredegar text is contained on folios 23r–125r. The other items in the manuscript are:

ff. 1r–5r: the Latin version of the *Life of Saint Symeon the Stylite*.

ff. 5r–6v: a *De Ortu et Obitu Patrum*. This is not the work of the same title by Isidore of Seville, but a set of 18 short accounts of patriarchs, from Adam to King David.

ff. 7r–22v: the illustrated *Physiologus* (facsimile in von Steiger and Homburger, 1964).

f. 125r (following the abrupt end of Fredegar): a lection (*Matthew* XVII. 1-9: the account of the Transfiguration).

ff. 125v–130r: a Latin sermon of Ephrem Syrus on the Transfiguration.[122]

2ᵇ London, British Library, Harley 5251 consists of 92 folios of 201 by 163 mm (165 × 115) in 12 gatherings, written in single columns of 24 or 25 lines to the page. The Caroline minuscule is thought to be that of a West Frankish scriptorium. Two folios are missing from the final gathering. Book divisions are incomplete. Book One receives a heading, as does Book Four, the abbreviated Gregory, which follows an 'explicit' for Book Three. However, no headings are to be found for either Book Two or Book Three, and the chapters of which they comprise are listed on the opening folios of the manuscript as if they were an integral part of the contents of Book One. On the verso of the final folio the truncated text of chapter 9 of the fifth book is followed by a magical invocation written in a different, darker, ink in a proto-Gothic hand.

3¹ and 3² The third class is represented by three manuscripts. The first of these was at some point split in twain, and is now divided between two libraries. The first section is Leiden, Bibliotek des Rijksuniversiteit, Vossianus Q. 5 (**3¹**), and the second is Vatican Library, codices Reginenses latini 713, folios 1–62v [of a total of 88] (**3²**).[123] The Leiden manuscript consists of 38 folios of 280 by 163 mm written in

---

[121] For a full description of the MS see von Steiger and Homburger 1964, 17–22. They discount the suggestion of Frederick M. Carey, 'The Scriptorium of Reims during the Archbishopric of Hincmar', in L.W. Jones (ed.), *Classical and Medieval Studies in Honor of Edward Kennard Rand* (New York, 1938), 41–60 at p. 57, that this was a Reims manuscript of the time of Archbishop Ebbo.

[122] These last two items relating to the Transfiguration, not formally recognized as a Feast in the western Church until 1457, might suggest a slightly later date for this manuscript, as liturgical calendars began to include it from the tenth-century onwards.

[123] *CLA* vols. X no. *108, and I no. 108; the other section of Vatican Reg. lat. 713 was written in the ninth-century, and hence is not described in *CLA*. For other illustrations of the script see Krusch edn facing p. 10. See Krusch 1882, 273–6; Wallace-Hadrill edition, l–li; Lindsay 1915, 460, 482, ascribing one section to St Gall and the other to Reichenau, while recognizing the two parts were originally a single manuscript!

single columns, normally of 28 lines to the page.[124] The opening folios of the manuscript, containing the first Book, have been lost. The Leiden section contains the Jerome and Hydatius epitomes, and the work of Julius Hilarian (ff. 28v–38r), and most of the preface to Gregory of Tours. The first 62 folios of the Vatican MS have an identical format, taking up the text where the Leiden section breaks off. The script is described by Lowe as being 'Alemannic minuscule' of the eight/ninth century, and he ascribes it to 'the St Gall-Reichenau area'. Bernhard Bischoff was more categorical in assigning the writing of the manuscript to the monastery of St Gall and giving it a date of c. 800.[125] There is a change of scribe in the Reginensis section between folios 26r and 26v. The compilation is divided into a five-book structure, but a number of changes have occurred in the contents. In all the manuscripts of this class the last three chapters of Book One are omitted and Julius Hilarian's *De Cursu Temporum* has been added, immediately preceding the epitome of Gregory of Tours.

3ª Lowe considered the next manuscript of Class 3, Vienna, Österreichische Nationalbibliothek 482, to be a copy of the Leiden/Vatican $3^1 + 3^2$, but Krusch and the modern editors have preferred to postulate the existence of a lost intermediary. The manuscript consists of 87 folios of 258 by 162 mm, all written in 23 single column lines per folio. Lowe considered it was 'written presumably at Reichenau and certainly in the Lake Constance region, to judge by the script', dating it to the late eighth or early ninth-century.[126] Otto Mazal opted more decisively for the end of the eighth-century, and Bischoff located its origin firmly at Reichenau.[127] The text of Fredegar here only extends to the end of the epitome of Gregory of Tours, on f. 86v. It includes the *De Cursu Temporum* of Hilarian (ff.59v to 61r). A late fifteenth-century copy, deriving indirectly from 3ª, now Augsburg Archiv des Bistums (formerly Bischöfliche Ordinariatsbibliothek) K 223, ff. 1–97v, forms the final example of the third class (**3ᵇ**).[128]

Although the earliest representative of Class 3, the composite Leiden-Vatican manuscript, 3^{1+2}, of c. 800, predates the extant codices of Class 4, the archetype of the latter has to date to no later than 768. Krusch and the other modern editors have seen the manuscripts of both of these classes as deriving their text of the seventh-century Fredegar compilation from a lost exemplar from Class 2 (the hypothetical 2^x), itself thought to be a generation removed from MS 1. However, the manuscripts of Classes 3 and 4 share the peculiarity of including Quintus Julius Hilarian's *De Cursu Temporum* in the Fredegar corpus; in the case of Class 3 this is placed in the middle of the compilation, while in Class 4 it replaces the *Liber Generationis* in Book One. It is hard to credit that such an addition of an uncommon text was coincidental. As the other textual changes and additions of new material are far more exten-

[124] de Meyier 1975, 15–17.

[125] *Karl de Grosse: Werk und Wirkung* no. 378, p. 218.

[126] *CLA* vol. X, no. 1480; see Krusch 1882, 276–8; Wallace-Hadrill edition, li (where it is ascribed to Mehrerau); for its illumination see Holter 1965, 100, Irblich 1993, 80–1, and Mazal 1981, 81.

[127] Mazal 1981, 81; Bischoff 1994, 37 and n.78.

[128] Krusch edition, 11, and *idem* 1882, 302–4.

sive in the manuscripts of Class 4, it would seem logical to postulate that the origi-
nator of the Class 4 manuscripts, probably the scribe or scribes working for Count
Childebrand in 751, derived both the text of the Fredegar compilation and knowledge of Hilarian's *De Cursu* from a manuscript of Class 3.[129]

4   Class 4 is principally represented by eight extant manuscripts; though Krusch,
followed by Wallace-Hadrill and Kusternig, postulated the existence of at least seven
lost intermediaries. However, the redating of a number of these manuscripts in the
course of recent decades must cast increasing doubt on the reliability of this area of
Krusch's *stemma codicum*. Changes in scribal practices and mere error may prove
better explanations for variations between these codices than the existence of complex patterns of missing intermediaries. In particular, MS London British Library
Harley 3771 (4^{b2}) was assigned by Krusch to the tenth-century and divided by him
from the archetype of Class 4 by five hypothetical manuscript generations. Redating
of the manuscript to the mid-ninth-century, making it one of the earliest extant exemplars of the class, makes such a complex descent look decidedly improbable.[130]
The *sigla* used by Krusch for this class of manuscripts will be retained here for
convenience of reference, but it must be admitted that they probably now bear little
contact with the actual relationship of the codices, which needs a full re-examina-
tion. Other notable manuscripts of this class include:
4^a   Vatican Reginensis lat. 213: this is assigned to the ninth/tenth centuries and is
thought to have been written in the monastery of S. Rémi, Rheims. It consists of
159 folios of 206 × 150 mm (165 × 115/20 mm), written in single columns of principally 20 lines per folio. (After f. 128v this varies between 21 and 25). As Wallace-
Hadrill pointed out, if Krusch was right in seeing it as the immediate ancestor of all
the manuscripts of Class 5 it must date to the ninth-century.[131] Certain confusion
has resulted from a claim by Ruinart in his edition of 1699 that he read the characteristic donor's inscription of the *Praepositus* Manno on a now lost folio. This would
seem to link the manuscript to a group of codices given by Manno to the monastery
of Saint Oyan in the Jura. This was said to be an error by S. Tafel in 1925, but is
still repeated by Wallace-Hadrill.[132] This manuscript lacks chapters 51–90 of
Fredegar's final book (here constituting Book Three), but it does have the Continuations. It also contains the 'Lorsch Annals' relating to the years 768–90, followed
by the *Annales Regni Francorum* for the years 791–806.[133] These are appended to
the Fredegar corpus without any divisions or headings.

[129] For the MSS of this work see Krusch, *MGH SRM* II, 220–9.

[130] Wallace-Hadrill edition, li, referring to a letter from Berhard Bischoff.

[131] Wallace-Hadrill edition, li. On the MS see Krusch 1882, 294–7; André Wilmart, *Catalogus
Bibliothecae Vaticanae: Codices Reginenses Latini* I, 502–4; Lesne 1938, 116; Tafel 1925, 50;
E. Pellegrin, 'Possesseurs des manuscrits latins du fonds de la Reine', *Revue d'Histoire des
Textes*, 3 (1973), 279.

[132] Tafel 1925, 50. A reference to such an inscription naming Manno in a 'Codex Juriensis'
of Fredegar can be found in a late seventeenth-century note at the foot of folio 126v of MS
Montpellier 158. The same note refers separately to this Reginensis manuscript.

[133] It is MS B3 in Kurze's classification of the manuscripts of the *ARF*: *MGH SRG* (Hanover, 1895), ix.

4^{ax} Troyes, Bibliothèque Municipale 802, folios 104r to 155r. Wallace-Hadrill, following Krusch, assigned it to Lorsch and dated it to the ninth/tenth centuries, but more recently Bernhard Bischoff has attributed it to Fulda and redated it to the first half of the ninth-century.[134] It contains only the first book of the revised (Childebrandine) Fredegar compilation, ending with the legendary account of Belisarius's defeat by 'Bucellinus'.[135] It has been rebound with a fourteenth-century manuscript of the works of Abelard.

4^{b1} Milan, Basilica di San Ambrogio, Archivio Capitolare M. 13: a late (?) ninth-century MS of which little notice has been taken.[136] It is written in a light brown ink in single columns with 27 lines to the page. The scribal hand has been assigned geographically to northern Italy and chronologically to the last quarter of the ninth century. There are some corrections in a greyish ink in a tenth century hand. The first folio is extraneous, being in double column format, though possibly from the same scriptorium as the rest of the MS, and containing conciliar acta. The revised Fredegar compilation in its three-book format is to be found on folios 2–142r. The divisions between the three books occur on folios 58r and 82v. Folio 142v is blank. Folios 143r to 144v contain four sketches, all in roundels, consisting of: (a) the months with their zodiacal signs, (b) the winds, (c) a map of the world, and (d) a depiction of the planets circling the earth, marked with the length in days of their respective cycles. On f. 145r begins chapter 1 (only) of Bede's *De Temporum Ratione*, which gives way on f. 147r to a text of the Latin version of Theophilus of Alexandria's *Ratio Paschalis*. This final section of the MS is much damaged; similarly, the text of Quintus Julius Hilarian, forming the first book of the revised Fredegar corpus, is heavily stained.

4^{b2} London, British Library, Harley 3771: as stated above this has been reassigned to the mid-ninth-century and to a western German scriptorium, possibly in Cologne, by the late Professor Bischoff.[137] A now erased (by use of reagents?) inscription on f. 2 reading 'Liber Sancti Panthaleonis in Colonia' indicates that it once belonged to the monastery of St Pantaleon in Cologne, founded by Archbishop Brun in the tenth-century. It consists of 145 folios of 262 by 175 mm (188 × 120), in 19 gatherings with quire numbers, having 24 lines to the page in single columns. One folio has been cut out between ff. 93v and 94r (modern numeration), which will have contained chapter 26 along with parts of chapters 25 and 27 of what recent editors call Book Four, but constituted Book Three in this class of manuscripts. There is a small

---

[134] Bischoff 1974, 67–8, 78–9, 102. It is bound together with a fourteenth/fifteenth-century MS of works of Abelard, and the codex once belonged to Paul Pithou. On this MS see Krusch 1882, 297–300.

[135] Krusch edition, 42–88.

[136] Krusch 1882, 300–1 (as with **4ax**, it is most unlikely that he saw this manuscript); Wallace-Hadrill edition, li, who misleadingly locates it in the 'Biblioteca della Basilica di San Ambrogio', i.e the Biblioteca Ambrosiana. The present account of it comes from the late Bernhard Bischoff's notes together with those of Walter Goffart, made as a result of their inspections of the manuscript in 1956 and 1979 respectively.

[137] Wallace-Hadrill edition, li–lii; also Krusch 1882, 301–2. For the erased inscription see *Catalogue of Ancient Manuscripts in the British Museum*, pt. II: Latin (1884), p. 85.

drawing of the bust of a bearded man on folio 1r. Seven lines of verse, some dam-aged, follow the Fredegar collection on folio 145v. The initial lines of this text have been erased, and the rest is lost. The bottom halves of both folios 1 and 145 have been cut off and replaced by blank pieces of vellum. Another MS, the fifteenth-cen-tury Munich clm 4352 (Krusch's 4^{b2x}), written in St. Ulric's monastery Augsburg (re-founded in 1474), is held to have been copied from the same exemplar as Harleian 3771, and was used extensively by Krusch who otherwise probably under-employed the manuscripts of this class in making his edition. However, it lacks precisely that section of the text that is missing in 4^{b2} due to loss of a folio, and so must be a copy of that MS and not of a common exemplar.

Among other relatively early manuscripts belonging to this class, which, however, have received less consideration in the formation of the critical editions may be mentioned:

4^{c1} Montpellier, Ecole de Médécine 158: dated to the tenth-century and with no certain provenance. Due to the loss of the final folio of the manuscript, the text concludes with the burial of Pippin in St Denis, having the contents of the final chapter added at the foot of the last folio in a probably late seventeenth-century hand. This manuscript consists of 135 folios of 252 by 168 mm (210 × 110/115), written in single columns of 26 lines each. Folio 1r contains a short genealogy of the French kings from 'Meroveus son of Priam' up to the twelfth-century in a hand of the lat-ter period. This might support a western Frankish origin for the manuscript. No other text is to be found in this codex.

On fol. 1v a full page initial I, decorated internally with interlace, has a facing, tonsured bust emerging from the top of it, flanked on both sides by a chimera, each holding in it's mouth the beginning of a canopy over the human figure, the top of which has been lost due to clipping of the edges of the manuscript. There is a col-our plate of this on p.12 of u. c. Nicq, G. Cames and G. Velay, *Les manuscrits de l'Ecole de Médécine de Montpellier* (Montpellier, 1994).

4^{c2} Paris, Bibliothèque Nationale lat. 4883A: This codex, consisting of 128 folios mainly in two columns, was seen by Krusch, who deduced an eleventh-century date for it from one of its component texts.[138] This is a privilege of Pope John XIX (1024–32) for the monastery of the Holy Trinity and St Pardulf at Arnac (diocese of Limoges), founded in 1028.[139] Krusch believed this was where the manuscript was written. The Fredegar collection, in three-book format, is found on folios 73–128, starting abruptly at chapter 18 of the Eusebius-Jerome Chronicle, and omitting chapters 38 to 79 of the epitome of Gregory of Tours. The text finally breaks off in chapter 44 of the Continu-

---

[138] On this manuscript see Krusch 1882, 306–9.

[139] Krusch thought the script used for this was an imitation Merovingian hand, but it is actually an attempt to copy the cursive used by the papal Curia: Philip Jaffé, *Regesta Pontificum Romanorum* (Leipzig, 1885), no. 4107. Walter Goffart notes that the text of this charter is in-serted into f. 67r without explanation, in the middle of a text here entitled '(Epistola) *Fulgentii ep(iscop)i ad Calcidium Grammaticum*'. The latter must actually be the *Expositio Sermonum Antiquorum* of Fulgentius 'the Mythographer'; see Rudolf Helm (ed.), *Fabii Planciadis Fulgentii Opera* (Stuttgart, 1970), 109–26. For the foundation of Arnac see *Gallia Christiana* vol. II (2nd edn Paris, 1720), 514.

ations, where the scribe writes: *Non repperio plus. Sufficiat igitur hoc.*[140] Other works found in this manuscript include Bede's *Chronica Maiora*, with chronological calculations extended firstly to 809 and then to 877, the probable date of a lost exemplar for at least this section of the codex, a Hebrew–Greek–Latin glossary, various letters and treatises of Jerome, and the *Satires* of Juvenal (in three columns).

4[c3] Leiden Rijksuniversiteit Voss. Q. 20, folios 1–8v.[141] This section of a composite manuscript is all that survives of a tenth-century codex written in double columns of 25 or 26 lines. Its present dimensions are 265 by 225 mm, and the script has been identified as being that of Tours. The second section, of 136 folios, is an early ninth-century, single column, Tours manuscript of Quintus Curtius Rufus, an abridgement of Orosius and the opening of Isidore's chronicle. The Fredegar section contains the abridged Jerome, commencing with its heading, Dares Phrygius (ff. 2v–6r) and the beginning of the epitome of Hydatius.

5 Class 5 is the most numerous in terms of surviving manuscripts but also the least important class, other than for its much expanded text of Gregory of Tours' *Libri Historiarum*. It would appear to have originated in the early ninth-century, possibly in the monastery of Lorsch, in consequence of the discovery of the fuller, though by no means complete, version of Gregory, to which it was made to serve as a continuation. All of the earlier parts of the Fredegar compilation, up to and including the epitome of Gregory of Tours, have been discarded. Only the section of original material relating to the period 584–741 has been preserved, and is added to the expanded text of Gregory as 'Book Ten'. As a manuscript of Class 5 (see 5[a] below) was used for the earliest printed edition, this is how Fredegar came to be treated from the sixteenth-century to the later nineteenth. The Class 5 text of the Continuations terminates with the death of Charles Martel in 741 (chapter 24 in the modern editions). In some of the manuscripts of class 'C' of the *Annales Regni Francorum* the text of chapters 11–24 of the Continuations has been taken from a manuscript of our Class 5, to serve as a bridge between a version of the *Liber Historiae Francorum*, which concludes in 721, and the *ARF*, which commence with the events of 741. As Class 5 has little value either for its text of what it keeps of the original Fredegar compilation or for that of the revised version of 751/768, the principal representatives are listed here with minimal comment.

5[a] Heidelberg Univ. Palat. lat. 864 ff. 110v–134v: eighth/ninth-century, written at Lorsch; containing some insular abbreviations. This was used for the *editio princeps* of Fredegar of 1568 (see editions below). See Bischoff 1974, 23, 66, 83–4, and 96. Krusch noted the text of this manuscript in the apparatus criticus of his edition, but did not otherwise bother with the Class 5 manuscripts.

5[ax] Paris, Bibliothèque Nationale lat. 5921: an eleventh-century copy of 5[a], made at or for St Arnulf, Metz.

5[xa] Berlin, Deutsche Staatsbibliothek lat. quart. 266: a tenth-century fragment, consisting of two folios containing Krusch's Book Four chapters 16 to 34 and 38 to 40, deriving from 5[a].

---

[140] Krusch 1882, 308–9; Wallace-Hadrill edition, lii.
[141] de Meyier 1975, 57–61; Krusch 1882, 309–10.

5ᵇ Paris, Bibliothèque Nationale lat. 9765, folios 100r to 110v: of ninth/tenth-century date, missing the list of chapters and the text of chapters 96 and 97; it was used by Wallace-Hadrill.

5ᶜ Saint-Omer, Bibliothèque Municipale 706, folios 116v to 144v: tenth/eleventh-century, written at the monastery of Saint-Bertin, in the suburbs of Saint-Omer. The manuscript was divided, and the other half of it is now MS Saint-Omer 697. The contents also include Eutropius, Marcellinus, the *Annales Regni Francorum* (Kurze's MS C3) and the *Annales Bertiniani*. It has been suggested that the latter two items come from a lost codex from the monastery of St. Vaast (Arras).

5ᶜˣ Brussels Bibliothèque Royale 6439–51: an eleventh-century copy of MS 5ᶜ, made at the monasteries of Lobbes or St Vaast (Arras).

5ᵈ Namur, Bibliothèque Publique, fonds de la ville 11: a ninth-century manuscript from the monastery of St. Hubert in the Ardennes; also containing Bede's *Historia Ecclesiastica* (MS 'N' of the Colgrave and Mynors edition: see *ibid.* p. xiv; Wallace-Hadrill gives a misleading location).

5ᵉ Brussels, Bibliothèque Royale 9361–67: twelfth-century from the monastery of S. Laurence, Liège.

5ᶠ Vienna, Österreichische Nationalbibliothek 473: late ninth-century, from NE Francia, possibly Saint-Amand, containing only the Continuations, together with the *Annales Regni Francorum* (henceforth ARF) and Einhard's *Vita Karoli* (MSS D1 and B1* of Kurze and Holder-Egger's editions). This manuscript was subsequently corrected against another close to MS 5ᵇ.

Excepts

A. Chapters 10 to 24 of the Continuations are also used to serve as an extension of the text of the *Liber Historiae Francorum* in a small group of manuscripts. These consist of:

5ˣ¹ St Petersburg F. Otd. IV, a tenth-century manuscript from Saint-Médard, Soissons, which it has been suggested copied a lost codex made for Charles the Bald (840–77). It also includes ARF (Kurze's C2), the *Annales Bawaricos Breves* (ed. Waitz in *MGH SS* XX, 8), Einhard's *Vita Karoli*, the anonymous *Vita Hludowici*, and a unique Carolingian genealogy (ed. Pertz, MGH SS XIII, 246).

5ˣ² Paris Bibliothèque Nationale lat. 10911, a ninth-century manuscript from Liège, which also contains ARF (Kurze's MS C1).

5ˣ³ St Gall 547, which has been given dates varying from the eleventh to the thirteenth centuries, and also includes Orosius, Paul the Deacon's *Historia Langobardorum*, Einhard's *Vita Karoli*, and Bede's *Historia Ecclesiastica*.

B. A small group of late manuscripts contain the text of what in Krusch's edition would be chapters 57 to 62 of Book Two, with the heading of *Gesta Theoderici Regis*, consisting of the legendary account of the Ostrogothic king Theoderic. These consist of MSS Vatican Reg. lat. 549 (twelfth century), Karlsruhe Badische Landesbibliothek Aug. V (twelfth century), Graz univ. fol. 454 (twelfth century), Vienna Nationalbibl. 428 (thriteenth century), Graz Univ. quart. 926 (a fifteenth century copy of Graz 454) and Vienna Univ. Bibl. 3334 (fifteenth century).

Stemma Codicum[142]

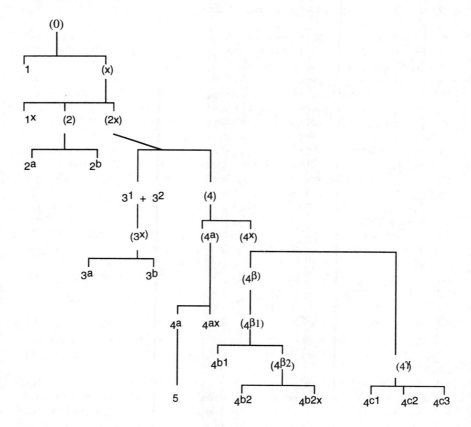

[142] From Krusch, as modified by Wallace-Hadrill; see his edition, liv.

Revised Stemma Codicum

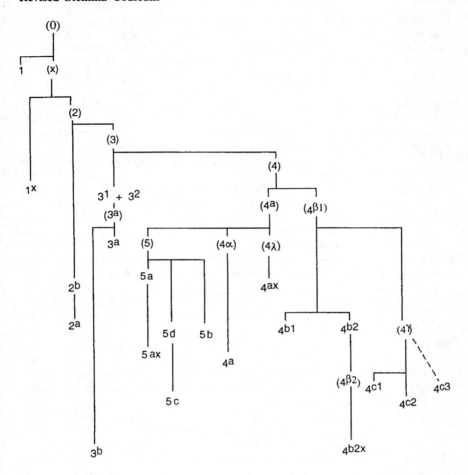

Editions

The fullest account of the editions of the work of Fredegar, up to his own day, is to be found on pages 345–51 of Krusch's article of 1882 and on pages 16–17 of his 1888 edition (see below). Unfortunately, the latter account in particular is marred by some typographic and other errors, and does not provide comprehensive bibliographic details on all the volumes cited. See also pp. lxii–lxiii of the Wallace-Hadrill edition of 1960.

Flacius Illyricus, Mathias: *Gregorii Turonici Historiae Francorum libri decem. Undecimus liber sive appendix Historiae Francorum, supplementi loco ab alio quopiam (Fredegario) Gregorio Thuronensi adjectus* (Basel, 1568). This used MS 5[a], and extended only to the end of ch. 24 of the Continuations; this edition was reprinted in Laurence de la Barre, *Historia Christiana Veterum Patrum* (Paris, 1583), and in the *Magna Biblioteca Veterum Patrum* vol. VI pt. 2 (Cologne, 1583 and 1618), in Marguerin de la Bigne, *Sacrae Bibliothecae Sanctorum Patrum* VII (Paris, 1589), 797–836, in Laurence Bochelle, *Gregorii Turonensis episcopi historiae Francorum libri decem* (Paris, 1610), and in the *Maxima Biblioteca veterum Patrum et antiquorum Scriptorum ecclesiasticorum* XI (Lyon, 1677), 815–30.

Canisius, Henricus: *Antiquae Lectiones ... tomus secundus* (Ingolstadt, 1602); reprinted in Andreas Schott, *Hispania Illustrata* IV (Frankfurt, 1608), 185–207, and with additional notes by Jacob Basnage in *Thesaurus Monumentorum Ecclesiasticorum et Historicorum, sive H. Canisii Lectiones Antiquae* (Antwerp, 1725), 147–226. This edition was largely, if not very accurately, dependent upon MSS 3[b] and 4[b2].

Scaliger, Joseph Justus, *Thesaurus Temporum, Eusebii Pamphili Chronicorum canonum omnimodae historiae libri duo, interprete Hieronymo. Item auctores omnes derelicta ab Eusebio et Hieronymo continuantes* (Leiden, 1606), using MS 4[ax]. Part of this was reprinted in Andreas Schott, *Hispania Illustrata* IV (Frankfurt, 1608), 208–12.

Freher, Marquard, *Corpus Francicae Historiae Veteris et Sincerae* (Hanover, 1613), 117–66 (bks III and IV, including the Continuations; using MSS 3[2] and 5[a]; reprinting the text of the Canisius edition for Continuations chs. 25–54).

André Duchesne, *Historiae Francorum Scriptores coœtanei* I (Paris, 1636), 722–8, using MSS 1 and 4[a] as well as the editions of Freher and Canisius.

Ruinart, Thierry, *Sancti Gregorii Turonensis opera omnia necnon Fredegarii Scholastici Epitome et Chronicon cum suis Continuatoribus* (Paris, 1699); reprinted in Maurice Bouquet, *Recueil des historiens des Gaules*, vol. 2 pt. 5 (Paris, 1738), and in Jean Pierre Migne, *Patrologia Latina* vol. LXXI (Paris, 1867), cc. 573–704. This edition used MSS 1, 4[c1], 5[a] and 5[ax], and was the most scholarly and critical to be published before that of Krusch in 1888.

Monod, Gabriel, *Etudes critiques sur les sources de l'histoire mérovingienne, deuxième partie: Compilation dite 'de Frédégaire* (Bibliothèque de l'Ecole des Hautes Etudes 63; Paris, 1885). This is a diplomatic edition of MS 1.

Krusch, Bruno, *Chronicarum quae dicuntur Fredegarii Scholastici Libri IV cum Continuationibus* in *MGH SRM* II: *Fredegarii et Aliorum Chronica.* (Hanover,

1888; reprinted 1984.), 1–193. This was the first modern critical edition, and is the only one to include the whole work. Although most of the manuscripts were used at some point or other in this edition, primacy was given throughout to 1, 2^a, 3, 4^{b2x} (a very peculiar decision), and 5^a.

Wallace-Hadrill, John Michael, *The Fourth Book of the Chronicle of Fredegar* (London, 1960). This is limited to what Krusch had designated 'Book Four' and to the Continuations, but is the first edition to recognize that MS 1 is not the direct ancestor of all the other extant manuscripts. Some use was made of additional manuscripts of Class 5, particularly 5^b.

Kusternig, Andreas, *Chronicarum quae dicuntur Fredegarii libri quattuor* in Herwig Wolfram (ed.), *Quellen zur Geschichte des 7. und 8. Jahrhunderts* (Darmstadt, 1982), 3–325. This omits Book I and chs. 1–52 of Book II. It derives from the edition of Krusch, as modified by Wallace-Hadrill.

The Wallace-Hadrill and Kusternig editions retain the four-book structure, with the probably non-authorial chapter divisions in the fourth book, largely because this had been adopted by Krusch. Although Wallace-Hadrill contemplated dropping the chapter divisions he refrained because this would 'have added to the difficulty of referring back to Krusch's edition and literature dependant upon it'.[143] Unfortunately, Krusch's edition represents a hybrid version of the work, of his own devising. He used a four-book structure because he thought this was the author's intention, although there is no manuscript justification for such a decision. On to this he added the new eighth-century material, the Continuations, from the manuscripts of Class 4, ignoring the facts that in this class a three-book structure had been used and that the contents of the entire compilation had been revised and altered. The resulting edited text is thus not true to any of the extant manuscripts. While Krusch was assiduous in collation and in producing a text that mirrored the deductions he was led to make about the relationships between the manuscripts, his edition, the only complete one, is flawed by the principles on which it was based and the initial decisions as to its intended contents and structure.

Translations

Claude Bonnet, Dauphinois, *L'histoire françoise de S. Grégoire de Tours. Augmentée d'un unzième livre* (Paris: Claude de la Tour, 1610).

de Marolles, Michel, *L'histoire des François de S. Grégoire evesque de Tours. Avec le Supplément de Frédégaire, écrit par les ordres de Childebrand frère de Charles Martel* (Paris, 1668), II, 745–876.

Guizot, François Pierre Guillaume, *Chronique de Frédégaire traduit en langue française* (Paris, 1823) in *idem, Collection des Mémoires* II, 163–265; revised with new appendices by Alfred Jacobs (1861).

Abel, Heinrich Friedrich Otto, *Die Chronik Fredegars und der Frankenkönige* (Berlin, 1849; 3rd edn revised by W. Wattenbach Leipzig, 1888).

---

[143] Wallace-Hadrill edition, lvii.

Wallace-Hadrill, John Michael, *The Fourth Book of the Chronicle of Fredegar* (London, 1960), facing the Latin text.

Haupt, Herbert, *Die Forsetzungen der Chroniken des sogenannten Fredegar* in Herwig Wolfram (ed.), *Quellen zur Geschichte des 7. und 8. Jahrhunderts* (Darmstadt, 1982), 45–325; facing the text of Andreas Kusternig's edition.

Secondary literature

Baudot, Marcel, 'La question du Pseudo-Frédégaire', *Le Moyen Age*, 29 (1928), 129–70.

Becher, Matthias, 'Drogo und die Königserhebung Pippins', *Frühmittelalterliche Studien*, 23 (1989), 131–53.

Becher, Matthias, *Eid und Herrschaft. Untersuchungen zum Herrscherethos Karls des Grossen* (Sigmaringen, 1993).

Becher, Matthias, 'Der sogenannte Staatsreich Grimoalds. Versuch einer Neubewertung', in Jarnut, Nonn and Richter (1994), 119–47.

Beeson, Charles Henry, *Isidor-Studien* (Munich, 1913).

Bischoff, Bernhard, *Lorsch im Spiegel seiner Handschriften* (Munich, 1974); 2nd edn *Die Abtei Lorsch* (Munich, 1989).

Bischoff, Bernhard, *Manuscripts and Libraries in the Age of Charlemagne*, tr. Michael M. Gorman (Cambridge, 1994).

Buchner, Rudolf, *Die Provence im Merowingischer Zeit* (Stuttgart, 1933).

Burgess, Richard W., *The 'Chronicle' of Hydatius and the 'Consularia Constantinopolitana'* (Oxford, 1993).

Cahen, Claude, 'Frédégaire et les Turcs' in *Mélanges offerts à Eduard Perroy* (Paris, 1973), 24–7.

Chaloupecky, Vaclav, 'Considerations sur Samon, le premier roi des Slaves', *Byzantinoslavica* 11 (1950), 223–39.

Chaume, Maurice, *Les origines du Duché de Bourgogne*, vol. I (Dijon, 1925), 1–72.

Chifflet, Pierre François, *Bedae Presbyteri et Fredegarii Scholastici Concordia ad Senioris Dagoberti definiendum monarchiae periodum atque ad primae totius Regum Francorum stirps chronologiam stabiliendam* (Paris, 1681), especially 331–53.

Collins, Roger, *The Basques* (Oxford, 1986), especially 91–7.

Collins, Roger, 'The *Vaccaei*, the *Vaceti* and the Rise of *Vasconia*', *Studia Historica*, 6 (1988), 211–23; reprinted with corrections in *idem, Law, Culture and Regionalism in Early Medieval Spain* (Aldershot, 1992), item XI.

Collins, Roger, 'Deception and misrepresentation in early eighth-century Frankish historiography: Two case studies', in Jörg Jarnut, Ulrich Nonn and Michael Richter (eds), *Karl Martell in seiner Zeit* (*Beihefte der Francia* 37: Sigmaringen, 1994a), 227–47.

Collins, Roger, 'Isidore, Maximus and the *Historia Gothorum*' in Scharer and Scheibelreiter (1994b), 345–58.

Dadinus Alteserra, Antonius, *Notae et observationes in X Libros Historiae Francorum beati Gregorii Turonensis Episcopi et Supplementum Fredegarii* (Toulouse, 1679), 378–94.

Delisle, Léopold, *Cabinet des manuscrits de la Bibliothèque Nationale* vol. III (Paris, 1881).

Demougeot, Emilienne, 'Les martyrs imputés à Chrocus et les invasions alamanniques en Gaule méridionale', *Annales du Midi*, 74 (1962), 5–28.

Drinkwater, John F., *The Gallic Empire: Separatism and Continuity in the North-Western provinces of the Roman Empire A.D. 260–274* (Stuttgart, 1987), 84–6.

Dupraz, Louis, 'Le premier duché de Bourgogne. Ses titulaires; leurs famille; leur politique', *Mélanges offerts à M. Paul–E. Martin* (Geneva, 1961), 19–37.

Erikson, Alvar, 'The problem of authorship in the Chronicle of Fredegar', *Eranos*, 63 (1965), 47–76.

Ewig, Eugen, *Die Merowinger und das Frankenreich* (2nd edn Stuttgart, 1993).

Fauchet, Claude, *Recueil des Antiquitez Gauloises et Françoises* (Paris, 1579); 2nd edn under the title *Les antiquitez Gauloises et Françoises. Augmentées de trois livres: contenans les choses advenuës en Gaule et en France, jusques en l'an sept cens cinquante et un.* (Paris, 1599); 3rd edn entitled: *Les Antiquitez et Histoires Gauloises et Françoises. Contenant l'origine des choses advenues en Gaule et les Annales de France depuis l'an du monde MMM.CCCL. jusques a l'an IX.C.LXXXVII. de Jesus Christ* (Geneva, 1611).

Ferrari, Mirella, 'La biblioteca de monasterio di S. Ambrogio: episodi per una storia', in G. Picasso (ed.), *Il Monasterio di S. Ambrogio nel medioevo. Convegno di studi nel XII centenario: 784–1984* (Milan, 1988), 82–164.

Fontaine, Jacques, 'King Sisebut's *Vita Desiderii* and the political function of Visigothic hagiography', in Edward James (ed.), *Visigothic Spain: New Approaches* (Oxford, 1980), 93–129.

Fouracre, Paul, 'Merovingian history and Merovingian hagiography', *Past and Present*, 127 (1990), 3–38.

Frei, Peter, 'Das römische Aventicum bei Fredegar', *Museum Helveticum*, 26 (1969), 101–12.

Fustel, de Coulanges, *Histoire des institutions politiques de l'ancienne France* vol. 3: *la monarquie franque* (Paris, 1888).

Ganshof, François Louis, 'L'historiographie dans la monarchie franque sous les Mérovingiens et les Carolingiens', *Settimane di studio del Centro italiano di studi sull'alto medioevo* XVII (Spoleto, 1970a), 631–750.

Ganshof, François Louis, *Een historicus vit de VIIe eeuw. Fredegarius, Mededelingen van de Koninklijke Vlaamse Academie voor Wetenschappen, Letteren en Schone Kunsten van België*, Kl. der Lett. 32 no. 5 (1970b).

Geary, Patrick J., *Aristocracy in Provence: the Rhône Basin at the Dawn of the Carolingian Age* (Stuttgart and Philadelphia, 1985).

Geary, Patrick J., *Before France and Germany* (Oxford, 1988).

Gerberding, Richard A., *The Rise of the Carolingians and the 'Liber Historiae Francorum'* (Oxford, 1987).

Gerberding, Richard A., 'Paris Bibliothèque Nationale latin 7906: an unnoticed very early fragment of the *Liber Historiae Francorum*', *Traditio*, 43 (1987), 381–6.

Goffart, Walter, review of Wallace-Hadrill edition of Fredegar in *Speculum*, 36 (1961), 692–5.

Goffart, Walter, 'The Fredegar problem reconsidered', *Speculum*, 38 (1963), 206–41; reprinted with addenda in *idem, Rome's Fall and After* (London, 1989), 319–54.

Goffart, Walter, 'From *Historiae* to *Historia Francorum* and back again: aspects of the textual history of Gregory of Tours', in *Religion, Culture and Society in the Early Middle Ages*, ed. Thomas F.X. Noble and John J. Contreni (Kalamazoo, Michigan, 1987), 55–76; reprinted in *idem, Rome's Fall and After* (London, 1989), 255–74 (with brief addenda).

Goffart, Walter, *The Narrators of Barbarian History* (Princeton, 1988).

Haag, O. 'Die Latinität Fredegars', *Romanische Forschungen*, 10 (1899), 837–933.

Hahn, A. 'Einige Bemerkungen über Fredegar', *Archiv für deutsche Geschichtskunde*, 11 (1858), 805–40.

Halphen, Louis, 'Une théorie récente sur la Chronique du Pseudo-Frédégaire', *Revue Historique*, 79 (1902), 41–56.

Hellmann, Siegmund, 'Das Fredegarproblem', *Historische Vierteljahrschrift*, 29 (1934), 36–92; reprinted in Helmut Beumann (ed.), *Ausgewälhte Abhandlungen zur Historiographie und Geistesgeschichte des Mittelalters* (Darmstadt, 1961), 101–57.

Hlawitschka, E. 'Karl Martell, das römische Konsulat und der römische Senat. Zur Interpretation von Fredegarii Continuatio c. 22', in *Die Stadt in der europäischen Geschichte: Festschrift für Edith Ennen*, ed. Werner Besch (Bonn, 1972), 74–90.

Holter, Kurt, 'Die Buchschmuck in Süddeutschland und Oberitalien', in Wolfgang Braunfels and Hermann Schnitzler (eds) *Karl der Grosse* III: *Karolingische Kunst* (Düsseldorf, 1965), 74–114.

Irblich, E., *Karl der Grosse und die Wissenschaft* (Vienna, 1993).

Jarnut, Jörg, *Agilolfingerstudien* (Stuttgart, 1986).

Jarnut, Jörg, Nonn, Ulrich and Richter, Michael (eds), *Karl Martell in seiner Zeit* (Sigmaringen, 1994).

Karl der Grosse: Werk und Wirkung (Aachen, 1965). Exhibition Catalogue.

Krusch, Bruno, 'Die Chronicae des sogenannten Fredegar', *NA*, 7 (1882), 247–351 and 421–516.

Krusch, Bruno, review of Lot, 'Encore la Chronique', in *NA*. 39 (1914), 548–9.

Krusch, Bruno, 'Fredegarius Scholasticus – Oudarius? Neue Beiträge zur Fredegar-Kritik', *Nachrichten der Gesellschaft der Wissenschaften zu Göttingen*, phil.-hist. Kl. (1926), pt. 2, 237–63.

Krusch, Bruno, 'Die handschriftlichen Grundlagen der Historia Francorum Gregors von Tours, pt. 2: Fredegarius – Oudarius?', *Historische Vierteljahrschrift*, 28 (1934), 15–21.

Kurth, Godefroid, 'L'histoire de Clovis d'après Frédégaire', *Revue des questions historiques*, 47 (1890), 60–100.

Kurth, Godefroid, *Histoire poétique des Mérovingiens* (Paris, 1893).

Lasko, Peter, *The Kingdom of the Franks* (London, 1971).

Leclercq, Jean, 'Un recueil d'hagiographie colombanienne', *Analecta Bollandiana*, 73 (1955), 193–6.